Th. Bentzon

The Condition of Woman in the United States

A Traveler's Notes

Th. Bentzon

The Condition of Woman in the United States
A Traveler's Notes

ISBN/EAN: 9783337205201

Printed in Europe, USA, Canada, Australia, Japan

Cover: Foto ©Andreas Hilbeck / pixelio.de

More available books at **www.hansebooks.com**

THE

CONDITION OF WOMAN

IN THE

UNITED STATES.

A Traveller's Notes.

By MADAME BLANC

(TH. BENTZON).

TRANSLATED BY

ABBY LANGDON ALGER.

BOSTON:
ROBERTS BROTHERS.
1895.

𝔘𝔫𝔦𝔟𝔢𝔯𝔰𝔦𝔱𝔶 𝔓𝔯𝔢𝔰𝔰:

JOHN WILSON AND SON, CAMBRIDGE, U.S.A.

CONTENTS.

———

BIOGRAPHICAL SKETCH OF MADAME BLANC.

WELL-KNOWN though the pen-name of Th. Bentzon may be, the charming woman who has made it one of the best loved and most respected names in contemporary literature, is far less so. She dislikes every attempt at publicity, and her works appear with no stir of trumpets. Reporters have never described her person or her parlor, and the boldest interviewer has never dragged from her an opinion on any subject. Outside her immediate circle, she exists only through her work. So when I came to Paris a few years ago, I was quite ready to believe, on the faith of a few imaginary accounts, that the pseudonym Bentzon belonged to a learned Frenchman living in Germany, a professor at some university beyond the Rhine. A little more love of notoriety would certainly have prevented such errors.

The fact is, that in Madame Blanc the woman of the world and the woman of taste came before the worker and professional writer who for some twenty-five years has never for a single instant lost interest in her art, who has produced more than a score of novels and tales and countless criticisms. She could not submit to the noisy puffery common in the literature of the day; the peculiarities which are so many tricks to attract attention, which amuse and stimulate vulgar curiosity, are contrary to her education and her nature; she therefore voluntarily renounced that portion of commonplace popularity which depends upon these indiscreet demonstrations. It is a sacrifice for which we need not pity her, since she has been rewarded by the respect and attachment of a select circle. No one has more friends or more devoted friends. She attracts and holds them, thanks to her steady cheerfulness, her gayety, the solid and brilliant charms of her conversation; thanks also to the charm of her vigorous and robust animation, shown without display, without great expenditure, but merely by the free, regular and harmonious play of her faculties. She produces in the highest degree the rarest impression which can be made by a modern woman, — that of a being in full possession of herself, perfectly balanced and perfectly healthy. It is the very grace of strength and moderation.

Like others, however, Madame Blanc has known the difficulties and the disappointments of a literary career; like others she might have hoarded up grudges had such been her humor, and if the obstacles and ill-will encountered at the outset ever left any sense of bitterness in those who conquer them by dint of persever-ance and courage. I think it was shortly before the war, that Madame Blanc, born de Solms, be-gan to write. The name Bentzon, then assumed by her, was the family name of her mother, to which she added her own Christian name Theresa, — Th. Bentzon, which some biographers have turned into the masculine name of Thomas, and others still more imaginative into Theodore.

An almost cosmopolitan education, which gave her a thorough knowledge of foreign languages and literatures, opened to the young girl a varied field of study and observation. Her first read-ing was done in English, and Walter Scott's "Waverley" caused the most vivid emotion of her childhood. Later on, vast insights into life and the world dawned upon her secluded youth. Without largely mingling with it, she entered the society of the end of the Second Empire; and together with her abstract culture, this asso-ciation, brief and involuntary as it was, furnished

her with a rich harvest of facts and experiences.
Nor was she without literary protectors. Her
father-in-law, Count d'Aure, equerry to Napoleon
III., was a friend of George Sand, whose support
he won for her, and who ever after felt the most
kindly and affectionate interest in her.

Under these circumstances, it seems as if she
had only to be seen to succeed. But — and this
may serve as a lesson to those who believe in
the supreme power of recommendations, and who
fancy that they are unjustly misunderstood,
while all barriers vanish before beginners who
have good backers — she had to struggle, she had
disappointments to endure; and when success
came, it was, as it always is, because she had
worked hard and asserted her talent.

Editors began to think better of this woman
whom they had considered too young, too fashionable, and ill-prepared for labor. Illustrated
papers, sporting journals, published some little
things from her pen. Her most important work
appeared in the "Revue Moderne," which had
a small circulation, and was but little read.
Still, one of her stories caught the eye of M.
Bertin, editor of the "Débats," who gave the
writer a commission. The work was finished
and delivered just as the war of 1870 broke out,

and the scene was laid wholly in Germany. However, the "Débats" had the courage to keep it, and to publish it in 1871.

It was afterwards published in book form by Hetzel, under the name of "Divorce." M. Buloz noticed it, and opened the pages of the "Revue des Deux Mondes" to Madame Blanc. Here she published "La Vocation de Louise," which began a long period of happy and fruitful production. "Une Conversion," "Une Vie Manquée," "L' Obstacle," "Tête Folle," "Désiré Turpin," "La Perle," "La Grande Saulière," "Georgette," and "Tony" appeared in rapid succession. All these stories were most favorably received by the public, and strengthened the reputation of their author. At the same time solid and brilliant sketches of English and American literature made Madame Blanc known in other countries. Now that she has gained the victory, she delights in looking back on those peaceful and busy years. Her mother, the Countess d'Aure, who lived with her, by her ceaseless care insured the quiet needful for work; she saw her son, destined to become a scholar and a famous explorer, grow to manhood. Everything smiled upon the stern choice which she made when she sought from her pen the dignity and security of her life.

The death of the Countess d'Aure introduced
a great grief into that happily organized existence. But here again Madame Blanc found comfort in her love of work, and in the regular
exercise of her art. It is since this bereavement
that she has given us her fine story of "Constance," — a strong and pathetic study of a
struggle with conscientious scruples in a delicately moulded soul. Some have considered it
as an argument against divorce; but the author
objects to all homilies. Her purpose was to show
the novel form imparted by recent social changes
to the struggle between duty and passion, between
personal instinct and a spirit of sacrifice. In a
soul as noble as that of Constance Videl, the
absolute — that is to say, goodness — very naturally triumphs. But if goodness be one and
indivisible, if it consist solely in conforming our
conduct to faith and the moral guidance which
we have accepted, it is by no means true that
this faith must of necessity be always the same.
Different creeds entail different duties. Divorce,
condemned by the Catholic Church, may be justified elsewhere. Nothing therefore matters save
loyalty and courage; and moral truth depends
wholly on the relation established between the
spiritual life and the practical life, and upon the

rigor with which it is maintained. Madame Blanc, whatever her religious ideas may be, never meant to say anything else; and we should fail to appreciate the meaning of her work, were we ·to claim for it any dogmatic character.

Setting aside all mental reservations of this nature, we may note an interesting fact, — a fact which bears not only on "Constance," but on all our author's novels. Madame Blanc has always been ranked with idealist writers; but her idealism, which is sometimes objective and poetic, as in that delicious revery known as "La Grande Saulière," is first and foremost subjective and moral idealism.

Let me explain. She is thoroughly familiar with men and life; and in the outlines of her characters, in the development of her plots, there is much of the splendid illusionism with which George Sand, for instance, confused all positive ideas. She knows the importance of social rank and of wealth, and takes these determinations of fact into account. There are cases where her perspicacity, her quick insight are such that she becomes almost a realist. Is there not realism of the saddest and also of the most powerful kind in "Tony," the story of the aberrations of M. d'Armançon, the country gentleman given over to drink and to the low empire of a covetous and crafty maid-servant? Jacqueline, one of Madame Blanc's latest heroines, is also full of terrible realism, with her girlish independence, her mental passion for a mature man, most truly and most carefully drawn. The constituent element, therefore, of Madame Blanc's idealism is not the nature of her observation, which is always calm and sensible, often bold; it is the firm control which she holds over the desires and passions impelling her heroes and heroines, the supremacy of the moral law, the invincible faith which we feel that she has in the higher destiny which all of us must needs work out, whatever the conditions of this material life may be, by the practice of virtue and the cultivation of the will, and consequently the healthy conscience shown by almost all these characters, at least of those who play the chief parts in her works. They are usually very varied, very real; they are most natural, neither too good nor too bad, but endowed with a great power of emotion, of prompt action, something both decided and mobile; their intensity of life and desire would render them very prone to err; they are able to sin as well as to do right. If they almost always avoid sin, it is therefore because they have faith and purpose, because an essential and permanent element governs the fantasies of their instinct and their visions. And their conscience partakes of the vivacity, the nobility, of their character; clear and decided, it has prompt and decisive reactions. Lucienne d'Armançon, who reaches the verge of crime before she finds repentance and regeneration in her very sin itself, in the intoxication of the crime which she was about to commit, is but a sort of synthesis of Madame Blanc's characters. Not one is passive, not one accepts his fate; they always react. They therefore produce a consolatory effect, in spite of their misfortunes or their faults. We feel that they possess a valor, a rectitude of feeling, which will cause them to conquer everything. They are never languid, or oppressed. The last thing to be found in her work — bright, kindly, and healthy as the mind which conceived it — is melancholy or nostalgia.

Great simplicity and great vigor of action result, in Madame Blanc's tales, from this strong moral constitution of her characters. As soon as her characters are settled, her story must be finished; indeed, these determined, free and yet well-disciplined creatures seem to move alone. And what makes them peculiarly interesting from this point of view is the fact that most of them are very young. Now, in France extreme youth, especially extreme feminine youth, does not exist, has scarcely any history. Look at the young girls in French plays, — all alike in dress and in conversation, with the same melancholy smile, the same speeches, the same airs of a wounded dove. Nothing personal, nothing distinctive, nothing that betrays individuality. The young French girl is naturally so cast into the shade that her timidity becomes a necessary ornament, as it were the outward sign of her moral qualities; the racial instinct of the French always leads them back to innocent simplicity as an ideal, and they cannot help believing in the virtue of ignorance and credulity. Here again Madame Blanc's cosmopolitan education shows itself. Before the day of Gyp, who has gone too far in her reaction, and whose Paulettes and Chiffons are really too emancipated and too free with their tongues, she created various living and natural figures of young girls, who are at the same time amiable and admirable. They have the graces of their sex and age; and they are also human beings, who accept their share of the struggles of fate, or are making ready for them. Perhaps they lack that first flower, that bloom of innocence, which pleases a certain dilettanteism; but it is questionable whether we are not mistaken in denying an entire class of beings the instinct and prescience of life; whether instead of creations which we wish to make ideally pure, we are not fashioning empty puppets; whether we are not clothing selfish and sometimes morbid fancies in the rosy garb of artless maidens.

I have already said that Madame Blanc's sketches of English and American literature have won her a brilliant reputation and many friends across the Channel and the Atlantic. She has several times visited England; and lately, friendly entreaties, and a desire to see with her own eyes a people whom she had long studied through their writings, led her to undertake a voyage to the United States. She spent several months there, and was everywhere received with open arms. The enlightened public of American cities greeted her with enthusiasm. She has brought back countless impressions and notes of her travels. She views her vast subject from a special point of view, and her work bears the modest title, "The Condition of Women in the United States." But in the United States woman is everything; while man confines himself to material tasks, trades and makes money, she represents the intellectual and artistic element, is at the head of all moral and charitable work. To take her as the objective point, therefore, is really to study the central point around which everything revolves. To be convinced of this, we have only to read what she says of the Woman's Building at the Chicago Fair, and above all her description of Hull House, a sort of phalanstery founded by Miss Addams in a suburb of the city, where the outcasts of fate find shelter, food, instruction, and amusement. Madame de Staël had a similar dream of a social order, where man was to keep the hard work for himself; while woman, free at last to cultivate her intellect and her soul, might become a sort of fairy distributor of goodness and beauty. She did not expect to see her splendid dream so quickly realized, and she would have watched its realization with passionate interest. Perhaps there are still some shadows to the picture; but Madame Blanc is too womanly, too merciful to her sex, thus far unprepared for the perfection of public virtues, not to throw a veil over them. It is for her to show us these manifestations of feminine personality and intelligence from their attractive side; and we can readily excuse her from showing us the faults.

MARIO BERTAUX.

THE CONDITION OF WOMAN

IN THE

UNITED STATES.

———•———

A TRAVELLER'S NOTES.

I.

FIRST IMPRESSIONS. — IN CHICAGO. — WOMEN'S
CLUBS.

Much has been written in regard to woman
in the United States. M. de Varigny has already shown us the source of her influence, in
a series of studies in the "Revue des Deux
Mondes." [1] In these studies he goes back to the
time when the heroic exiles who came over in
the "Mayflower" helped their fathers and their
husbands to build the primitive cabin destined
to serve alike as church and school. The equals
of man, from the first, they became his superiors
— so it seems — by intellectual culture and

[1] March 15, May 15, September 1, 1889.

refinement. While the head of the family devotes himself wholly to business, they personify at his side — or far from him, for the household is often divided — elegance, pleasure, and luxury. We know these American women through meeting them in Paris, and we see them at the first glance in New York. Possibly, all women of fashion, whose idle existence is spent in great capitals, watering-places, winter resorts, and gay seashore hotels, are all cut out much after the same pattern. Without any real originality, each of them represents that cosmopolitan society which has no native land. Their essentially artificial type has figured to excess in novels and plays; we have no desire to recur to it. But side by side with millionnaires and professional beauties, in America as elsewhere, there is a far more numerous class, concerning which much less has been said, — a class corresponding to the better part of the French middle classes. If you tell me that there are no classes in the great republic, I can but reply that this is a mistake. Besides the brutal distinctions established by the greater or less amount of dollars, we soon discover an infinity of degrees created by birth, surroundings, and education. To know America thoroughly it is not enough to gaze at this or that wandering star: we must frequent the best society of Boston, New York, and Philadelphia; we must visit the Southern States so sorely tried by war; we must penetrate the remote farms of the West; in short, we must study woman in the far-distant corners of that continent made up (not to mention the territories) of forty-four States, not one of which is so small as Switzerland, and some of which are much larger than France. To form a final judgment without making this preliminary inquiry, is almost as absurd as to hold all European women in light esteem. Americans of North, South, West, and East have nothing in common but certain traits which they owe to their common school education and their familiar acquaintance with liberty. It struck me that the best way to mark the differences would be to set down accurately the notes taken from day to day during a journey of several months' duration, — a woman's notes about everything that relates to the condition of women.

The moment is favorable, since the important question of extending the right of suffrage to a sex which already possess so many privileges is just now more than ever the subject of debate before the legislatures of the Union. As we all know, women have for sometime been allowed to

vote in Wyoming; in 1889 they obtained the
right of municipal suffrage in Kansas; so also,
I believe, in Colorado; in half the other States
they cast their ballots in all matters pertaining
to schools and to public instruction. It now
depends upon their own will to advance far
beyond this point. Incautiously directed, the
woman question may become as embarrassing as
the immigration or the negro question; and with
all possible prudence, there can be no half way
measures! Let us therefore consider it at the
most favorable moment. Moreover, the notes
which follow, although jotted down at odd intervals, may still possess the merit of throwing some
light on the future fate of our Old World. The
New World has already borrowed many good
things from us; it gives us back in return others
which contain a strange mixture of good and evil.

.

Types and Aspects.

American society was represented in abstract
on the boat which bore me from Havre to New
York, causing much amazement and many errors
on the part of such as were not yet familiar with it.

There was a scornful and very elegant group
of American Anglomaniacs, — those Americans

whose compatriots declare that they turn up their trousers on Broadway in fine weather because it is raining in London; servile copyists of English fashions, bearing, and manners, more or less apt efforts to assume the supercilious arrogance and systematic exclusiveness which befit the representatives of aristocracy. The women walk the deck in cloth gowns knowingly cut by the most famous tailor in London, their hands in their pockets with the free and easy air of a lady visiting her stables before she mounts her horse. All the young men are carefully shaven as befits New York dudes; they condemn their face to utter impassivity, affect sporting slang and a mirthless, jerky laugh, with the pronunciation of modish Englishmen who drop a letter in talking, just as the same set in France mercilessly suppress all connectives. I think I can guess that these Americans have never done anything but spend abroad the fortune painfully acquired by their fathers in some form or other of trade: but my ignorance is enlightened. I stand in the presence of the purest of blue blood, of so-called Knickerbocker families. That large lady, for instance, who scarcely ever leaves her stateroom, figures among the Four Hundred in New York. I need say no more.

I have now the measure of the social divisions
which exist in the land of equality. To cope
with the insolence of newly-won wealth, one must
be able to point to pre-Revolutionary ancestors,
or at least to ancestors who distinguished themselves during the Revolution. Those who can
boast of a Dutch or Swedish name established in
the country before the English rule, feel all the
pride of a Rohan or a Montmorency; and even
those who do not possess these great advantages
hasten, as soon as possible, on any pretext whatsoever, to draw the line as distinctly as possible
between themselves and common mortals. Hence
a very droll statement, such as abound in the land
of humor: "Since the line absolutely must be
drawn somewhere, many people draw it at their
own father." Never, until I went to America,
did I understand how humiliating it may be to
bear the name of Smith or Jones.

The great personages of our boat form a party
by themselves. They seem determined to make
no acquaintances. At the utmost, now and then,
the men, less absolute than the other sex in the
matter of prejudices, descend from their pedestal
to chat with some pretty woman. Among these
latter is a young girl. She cannot smile without
showing alluring dimples; accordingly she smiles

continually. She is dressed like a picture, in the style suited to a long voyage; she seems to find universal favor. I do not discover until we land that she is a mere shop-girl. In the South, more than one daughter of a good family, ruined by the war of secession, is forced to work for a living. This piquant brunette is from Louisiana; she earns a large salary in one of the chief shops of New Orleans. During her vacation she visited Hungary (the home of her ancestors), Germany, and France. She has read plenty of French novels. Southern shop-girls pride themselves on their literary tastes; some of them are said to write for local magazines. Miss —— professes a sincere worship of George Sand, despite the air of reserve assumed by some of our passengers at the sound of that name. "But," she says, waxing eloquent in regard to "Consuelo," "her heroines are too perfect; it is enough to discourage any one from trying to be virtuous." And the dimples appear at the corners of her rosy lips. Here, indeed, are great reverses cheerfully endured.

Nothing can be prettier than to see the young girls walk the deck, arm in arm, escorted by admirers of various ages, whom they never seem to discourage very severely, — no powder to be

affected by the salt air, abundant tresses which
the wind may release without danger beneath the
Tam-o'-Shanter or the naval cap which are almost
universally worn.   Even the old ladies have them
planted on their scanty locks, although they are
less becoming to them.

Let us confine ourselves to the young girls.
They are for the most part slender, erect, almost
all tall, — height being fashionable in New York
society, whose edict rules, and women, as we
know, always finding some way to adapt themselves to the fashion at any cost. Some show
signs of what they call "nervous prostration."
They lack the robust British health, nor have
they usually the regular features of the fair
English girl; and although certain New England
damsels reminded me of Greek statues retouched
by the hand of an esthete, we must admit that
in the West the mixture of races often produces
types of but little distinction. The shape is
seldom perfect, however smart the appearance
may be; there is too much fragility, too much
thinness. In an assembly of women in low-cut
dresses, the French woman would surely have
the advantage; therefore she bares her shoulders
more freely. But the Americans are as quick
witted, and as graceful as any women in the

world. Those on the steamer, as a rule, talk
freely with all the men, — the only exception
being a negro gentleman from Hayti, who stalks
about in melancholy silence wearing a Greek fez
embroidered in silver. But there is nothing bold
or shocking in their coquetry. If, instead of
being young girls, they were so many young
married women, we should think their conduct
quite correct; it is a mere question of the point
of view. Their perpetual motion, their airy
lightness, remind me of the gulls continually
soaring about the blue or cloudy sky, swooping
down now and then to the foam-crested waves,
and again resuming their capricious flight. So
too these damsels occasionally sink upon their
steamer-chairs, arranged in sheltered corners well
suited to conversation. The deck stewards bring
up their luncheon, which they eat with a good
appetite while they watch a passing vessel or the
sunset.

Sometimes I am struck by their lack of percep-
tion in regard to culinary matters. I hear them
ask for sardines and lemonade; mixtures which
strike a Frenchman as incongruous are in high
favor. But usually they seem to appreciate the
excellent fare of the transatlantic steamers; and
it seems to me that the members of temperance

societies who vaunt their principles so loudly as soon as their foot is on their native soil, yield a point here in favor of the red and white wines which are so freely offered. "The Yankees are as great hypocrites as the English, to say the least," said one of my fellow-countrymen met by chance; "when they refuse to drink wine with virtuous excuses, they get drunk on whiskey at the bar. In reality their coarseness goes beyond everything, you'll see; they are always spitting in every direction, and they are ignorant of the most elementary use of the handkerchief! As for the famous flirt, she often goes, you may be sure, to the last extreme. In hotels and restaurants there is always a special door for ladies. . . . Nonsense! in spite of this absurd precaution, friends meet on the other side again, and the devil is no loser. . . ."

I take leave to suggest to this well-informed gentleman that the purpose of the ladies' entrance, which is quite a convenience, may not be merely to create an absolute separation between the two sexes. Moreover, I cannot help thinking that he must be somewhat like the traveller who wrote in his note-book, "At Tours, all the women have red hair," because one red-haired woman passed him in the street. We French have a

passion for conclusions and generalizations. If
I were to take everything literally which this
fellow tells me, I should believe that there are
no more interesting establishments in America
than the bar-rooms paved with dollars; that all
Americans, without exception, talk through their
noses; and that their daughters are ready to do
anything for the sake of getting married.

As for the famous nasal twang, we soon learn
that it does not exist, at least to any disagreeable
extent, among well-educated people; and daily
experience shows us, even on the steamer, that
the much accused flirt may be ingenuous enough
after all.   After being scandalized by the glances,
the smiles behind a fan, the airs and graces of all
sorts directed like a well-fed fire by one of our
young fellow-passengers at a visibly enamoured
gentleman, did I not discover that this guilty conversation was nothing but an innocent game.
Instead of talking of their own affairs, they were
asking each other conundrums! The Sphinx
took the greatest delight in tormenting her victim; but the whole world might have listened
and heard no harm, despite the evidence of our
eyes.   And even when appearances are plainly
shocking, we must beware of a frequent source
of error: the most vulgar of American women is

as well dressed as the most aristocratic. I saw
in New York a woman who sold newspapers, who,
aside from her business, looked like a lady, and
was, it seems, distinctly an honest creature, in
spite of the frantic coquetry which led one to
suspect her of anything and everything.   But the
honesty like the coquetry of a woman who sells
newspapers may be of indifferent delicacy.   The
flirtations witnessed in hotels and restaurants, in
cars or on steamboats, may often have damsels of
a`like category for their heroines, — the indepen-
dence of fashionable young girls, their free and
undaunted manners, often leading all but the
most clear-sighted observer into blunders.   For
instance, on board ship, Miss X. was travelling
alone; one day she asked the librarian for some
French books; she chose two, "Fromont Jeune
et Risler Aîné," and "Mademoiselle de Maupin,"
then turning to a young man who was passing,
she asked his opinion in regard to her purchase.
And here I admire the respect shown on all
occasions by the American men to a woman even
if unknown.   The young man blushed up to his
eyes as he read the title of Théophile Gautier's
masterpiece, but merely said, —

   "This one, by Daudet, is a good book; as for
the other — "

"Wicked? So much the better!" interrupted the mischievous girl laughing aloud, and she fled, bearing off her booty, which she brandished with an air of defiance.

Is this perversity? Is it innocence,— the innocence of Daisy Miller, so marvellously painted by Henry James that his compatriots have never forgiven him? Who knows?

The *demi-monde*, strictly speaking, does not exist in America; nevertheless, there must be between self-respecting women and a certain unmentionable social scum a third category, — the numerous category of more or less yielding, more or less rakish, coquettes. These are sought by many foreign travellers. Hence general statements in regard to the American flirt, only equalled in absurdity by the fabulous tales which circulate in America in regard to the adultery, almost inseparable from marriage, as described by French novelists. The truth is that women, when they are what is amiably styled "light," become so in America before marriage and in Europe afterwards; but on both sides of the Atlantic there are many more irreproachable maidens and perfectly faithful wives than is believed on either shore. This statement is not new, but it can never be repeated too often.

THE WORLD'S FAIR: THE WOMAN'S BUILDING.

I was one of the latest comers at the World's Fair; therefore I can only give the bewildering impression, the dream-like memory produced by two or three hasty visits. Our exhibitions had not prepared me for anything of the sort. I do not doubt that they were more complete, more perfect in detail; but they did not attain to that sum total of effect which in my memory partakes somewhat of the mirage, — a mirage which vanished instantly after the first dazzle, as every truly magical apparition should vanish. I had scarcely time to see the princess in her attire woven of sunbeams, which the next instant was but rags and tatters. Never did a metamorphosis occur so swiftly, save in the story of Cinderella. The knell of the Fair was sounded on October 31; the next day nothing was left but the orderly tumult of a colossal removal. At the first cold blast of autumn, solitude took up its abode in that magnificent court of honor, where for the space of a summer, delegates from every quarter of the globe had assembled, amid feasts and spectacles. Actors, or supernumeraries, hastened to salute the full triumph of the most enchanting thing on earth, — youth, even if it have but that fugitive lustre which we call the "*beauté du diable.*" This undoubtedly was somewhat the order of the beauty of the countless palaces which, after giving us the illusion of marble, crumbled into dust when they were not destroyed by fire; but what matters it, if during their brief existence they rivalled Venice, reflected in the mirror of lagoons traversed by flat gondolas? I do not care to know just what they contained; it displeased me to think that they had a useful purpose, any purpose whatsoever. I only know that the Adriatic is no more beautiful than Lake Michigan, and that the inspiration of genius once evoked upon that boundless blue sheet the snows of a phantom city, swift to fade away into the blue of heaven.

Next to the poetry of that ephemeral apparition of Greece, Italy, and the age of Louis XIV. in the American West, nothing was more interesting than the attitude assumed in view of it by the countless sight-seers, collected from all parts of the New World. Their admiration showed itself in absorption. There we became acquainted, after studying the most diverse specimens, with a people strangely master of itself and its emotions. The decorum with which, if need be, it lynches without passion criminals whom the law does not touch, is amply explained by its grave attitude when at play. Europeans, more expansive and more turbulent, think its aspect gloomy, and are wont to deem it dull. But this dumb herd enjoys things in its own way. A farmer from the far West became, in my hearing, the eloquent interpreter of the great majority, expressing his deep and restrained enthusiasm in almost biblical language. What he expressed, others felt; they must feel it more than ever in intense memory, now that they have returned to their various States. Visions similar to those of the apocalypse, the paradisal splendors of a new Jerusalem illumined by changing electric lights and bedewed by luminous fountains, doubtless follow them into those toilsome tasks of clearing the ground so well depicted by the poet pre-eminent of the prairie, Hamlin Garland: "They plough, they sow; they feed the soil with their own life, as the Indian and the buffalo did before them."

Having done justice to the general effect of the White City, I feel I have the right to add that it contained more than one structure in bad taste, and that the Woman's Building in particular failed to strike me as a masterpiece. That villa of the Italian renaissance, crowned by angels

with outspread wings, has been praised even to
hyperbole for its feminine qualities "of reserve,
delicacy, and distinction," — wholly moral qualities, which may not suffice when it is a
question of striking out from the stone an idea,
be it great or small. In point of fact, Miss
Sophia Hayden, of Boston, a graduate of the
Massachusetts School of Technology, who came
off victorious from a national competition open
to all ambitious aspirants of her sex, did not
succeed in proving that architecture is one of the
arts in which the woman of our day shines. Nor
were the decorative groups of her collaborator, a
young Californian, Miss Rideout, of the highest
order. I might say the same of the paintings
in the hall of honor. Certainly women understand decoration and ornament as well as and
better than any one, but on condition that they
hold aloof from the two ambitious regions of
statuary and fresco. And yet Mrs. MacMonnies,
Lucia Fairchild, the Misses Sherwood, Emmet,
Brewster, and Sewell are not wanting in talent;
and indeed Mary Cassatt, well known in Paris,
where some of her etchings figure in the Luxem-
bourg collection, has a great deal. Still, they
all make a mistake to venture into the domain of
Puris de Chavannes. I will merely allude to the

very characteristic fashion in which Miss Cassatt conceives the subject " Modern Woman " as opposed to " Primitive Woman,"— her lowly labors, her subjection to man, her mission as a mother and a beast of burden, all recounted to us by Mrs. MacMonnies on a sixty-foot space of wall. The central part of the panel represents the daughters of Eve in modern fashionable dress, in an orchard, busily gathering, in hundreds, the fruits of the tree of knowledge, of which their more modest ancestors stole but one. To the left, a flying figure of Glory is pursued by women, their hair floating loose, their arms outstretched, a flock of ducks at their heels. To the right a young woman lifts her skirts with an audacious gesture, just ready to dash into Loie Fuller's dance, while two of her companions, seated on the grass, watch her, one of them playing on a stringed instrument. It is needless to say that Miss Cassatt is of the new school. Degas, Whistler, and Monet are, it seems, her gods. But, after all, she is herself; and the merit of individuality can be attributed to but very few American painters, men or women. Often very strong in regard to technique, they have thus far been incapable of freeing themselves wholly from the influence of their French or German masters.

Many aspirants to high art would do better to excel in flower-painting, like Miss Greene, of Boston; to distinguish themselves in portrait-painting or in water-colors, like Mrs. Sarah Sears, of the same city. Another Boston woman, Mrs. S. W. Whitman, is also deserving of praise. She does not disdain to apply her great artistic gifts to the designing of exquisite book-covers for publishers, or to the composition of beautiful glass, without detriment to more serious tasks. She has profited much by the experiments made by the chief of American painters, John La Farge, to whom his country and the world owe the renewal of the art of making glass windows, some fifteen years ago. He discovered the logical use of lead, which in ancient glass was merely an ugly necessity, and made it an element of decorative beauty, — so utilizing it for the outline of his figures as to imitate the irregular touch of the brush, while surprising effects were obtained by means of glasses of various colors fastened one over the other in such a way as to increase the depth and breadth of tone, or to modify the transparency. Mr. La Farge then conceived the idea of using fragments, thought defective, of that opalescent glass made in America in imitation of porcelain. The heads and hands alone still have to be painted, in this translucent mosaic held together by lead instead of cement, since for flesh, expression is requisite. We have seen John La Farge's glass at French Exhibitions, where their author's merit has been loudly acknowledged.

The triumphs won in this branch of industrial art has excited great rivalry; hence all the designs and sketches for glass to be seen at Chicago.

The illustrations for books and magazines by women struck me as interesting. I may mention Mrs. Mary Hallock Foote, who, handling the pencil as skilfully as the pen, embellishes her own stories with drawings which are highly appreciated. As china decorators American women are decidedly inferior to the French, although the Cincinnati Pottery Club send promising specimens. On the whole, the professional schools of industrial art in America are still far from equal to the French, in spite of their steady progress. The school of embroidery scarcely dates back seventeen years: it prospers, encouraged by lively patronage; but its workwomen lack what we have in France, — stimulating competition with women of the best society, who do not scorn to devote themselves to certain kinds of manual labor and to convert them into art. It

was enough to look at the small room reserved
for the work of French ladies to note this difference. Very many American women despise the
needle; dressmakers and milliners told me how
hard it was for them to find workers even at high
wages. The teacher's diploma is the objective
point which turns them away from everything
else.

. To go back to the Woman's Building. It is
not there that we find the strongest evidences of
talent. In every land women make a mistake
when they herd together by themselves to exhibit
their work. Competition with man is indispensable for the elimination of rubbish, and also to
set forth, not always the inequality, but the profound difference in the gifts and aptitudes of the
two sexes. This does not imply that I blame the
idea itself of the building. Its halls for meetings, for organization, etc., did great service,
sheltered the congresses and associations of
women, and all the various movements directed
by women. All who had, or thought they had,
new ideas to express, found a hearing. As for
women musicians, either professional or amateur,
a jury chosen by the national committee on music
determined whether or no each lady should take
part in the concerts given during a period of six

months,— the fact of appearing on the programme conferring lasting distinction. We were thus enabled to gauge the rapid and increasing development of musical taste in America. Fine voices are common there, although they have long been reproached with a lack of soul; and instrumental music is cultivated with the earnestness and persistence brought to bear on their studies by American women, who are least content of all women in the world with what are called "accomplishments." They may have lacked the gift of feeling, which is independent of a desire to learn; it was however developed years ago by the German influence prevailing in many cities, and by weekly classical concerts scrupulously attended. A large share of the merit due for this education belongs to Mr. Theodore Thomas, director of the Section of Music at Chicago.

The material interests of poor exhibitors were not neglected in the Woman's Building. Every variety of article made by feminine hands found a market there, thanks to very profitable sales; and cooking lessons were given daily, a matter of inestimable value in a country where it seems the exception for a woman to be born a good housekeeper. Up to the last the Woman's Building was the very expression, if we may say so, of the broadest hospitality. The Children's Building, its natural annex, enabled mothers of families to leave their little ones in the best of care while they visited the exhibition, and the children themselves to learn a great deal while they played, for there were lectures and shows and a library suited to their understanding. Nothing was better worth seeing than the working of the Kindergarten and the kitchen-garden belonging to it. Miss Huntingdon, of New York, who established the latter, directed classes where little ones played at making a bed, at sweeping and dusting, and were thoroughly taught every detail of housekeeping.

When we think of the vast task accomplished by the lady managers in arranging these complex manifestations of feminine progress, in the space of six months, we feel that we can hardly say too much in praise of the committee headed by a star of Chicago society, Mrs. Potter Palmer, who had hitherto enjoyed a reputation only for beauty, elegance, and wealth, but who at once rose to the full magnitude of the task allowed her. Committees of ladies had already contributed largely to the success of the two great exhibitions at New Orleans and Philadelphia, but the distinctive

feature of the World's Fair was the official intro-
duction of women on the jury, admitted once for
all to protect their own interests.   They did their
work with remarkable intelligence.   Let us over-
look the petty discussions, the petty rivalries,
which, if we are to trust the revelations of an
indiscreet press, arose between certain delegates
from various States; this does not lessen the
proofs of devotion and zeal afforded by the
majority, or the final result attained.   The
avowed object of the exhibition was to permit
women to help one another, and each one of
them to help herself; it also aimed to give a
clear and precise idea of the universal condition
of woman in our day.   This double end was attained.   By the way, the set statistics sent from
Paris showing in eighteen tables, the part played
by French women in agriculture, trade, administration, education, the liberal professions, economy, etc., were more complete than any other,
and will certainly serve as a model for any future
lists of this sort.

Let us note one very happy innovation: every
manufacturer was asked to say whether his exhibit
was wholly or in part the work of women, thus
insuring to each her share of praise.   The committee suggested this; they also proposed many

other valuable things which will endure. Those who may wonder at the experience displayed in such matters by a group of fashionable women, do not know what a school in organization the clubs to which they belong are for American women. I shall have frequent occasion to refer to them, as I travel from one city to another with my readers.

WOMEN'S CLUBS.

The first women's clubs were established some twenty-five years ago almost simultaneously in Boston and New York. From that time on, under the protection of these two great centres, especially the former, similar associations have continually arisen in the various States. They now number more than three hundred, and the General League which embraces them all lends them new strength. Those of Chicago are particularly active. I visited the two principal ones, — the Fortnightly and the Woman's Club.

The Fortnightly is exclusively a literary club. I found it established in elegant rooms, in the Hotel Richelieu; women of all ages, in street dress, were seated in large numbers before the platform occupied by the president and two

members of the committee. Mrs. Amelia
Gere Mason, well known through her book on
"Women of the French Salons," read a paper
called "Old and New Types of Women," — a
subject chosen according to the usual custom and
discussed later, objections being raised, details
added, or errors corrected. I admired the ease
of manner shown by all the ladies who spoke in
turn, the precision of their opinions, the critical
sense which they displayed. They will certainly
enter Congress well prepared to reason con-
secutively and to discuss calmly, — the thing
which women of all countries are least able
to do. But few compliments were paid; there
was no desire to be agreeable, not the least hesitation to speak what they felt to be the truth,
even if the truth were an unpleasant one. I was
equally struck by the good temper of the essayist
thus exposed to a cross fire. It is evident that
periodical meetings of this nature have a strong
influence on the mind of women, on their powers
of conversation, banishing frivolous and too personal subjects, accustoming them to listen atten-
tively, to refute an argument logically. At the
same time the studies required in advance on the
most various subjects relating to morals, philosophy, science, and history, sometimes reveal
genuine literary ability.

After the meeting, tea is served; people walk about and talk. One of the members of the club, who has spent much time in France, is kind enough to tell me that, after Chicago, she considers our "little Paris" incomparable! I am introduced to a number of people who politely reproach me for refusing to make a speech, all strangers present at the meeting having been invited to take the floor. When I reply that I am wholly unaccustomed to speaking in public, they assume the pitying air that the Turkish ladies wore when they found that Lady Mary Wortley Montague was imprisoned in a corset, or which we might ourselves wear on looking at the maimed foot of a Chinese woman. I tell the president that the American clubs bid fair to rival the old salons of France, so great is the wit displayed; only, their doors are closed upon men, while the sole purpose of our salons was to gather them together and help them to shine, — upon which she merrily answers, though with a strange flash in her eyes, "Oh, as for that, we don't care; we prefer to shine on our own account!" And the husbands, brothers, and sons bear them no grudge. They think it delightful to come home after a day devoted to business, and be told by their womankind of all that is going on in the world of leisure; the women skim the reviews, the books, and the news for the benefit of the men.

Among the women present who attract me at first sight is one of the notabilities of Chicago, — Dr. Sarah Stevenson: there are at least two hundred women doctors in the city, but she has the largest practice. She is president of the Woman's Club, whose programme is far broader than that of the Fortnightly, and which is especially devoted to social reforms. Dr. Stevenson talks eagerly to me of what she considers the greatest achievement of the women of Chicago, — the establishment of a protective agency for women and children. The object of this association is to guard their rights; to enforce the payment of wages unjustly withheld from working-women or servants; to prevent exorbitant rates of interest on loans and the violation of contracts; to find homes for foundlings, take children from unworthy parents, and procure a divorce for wives who are maltreated; to uphold a mother's right to her children, etc. A lawyer is appointed by the society. All that she tells me awakens my liveliest interest.

I go on the day fixed to the pseudo-Roman structure still known as the Art Institute, although another edifice of classic style has risen within a year on the lake shore, on Michigan Boulevard, to hold the art collections of the city. In a vast hall, the seats, rising one above the other and forming an amphitheatre, are already covered with women whose appearance and dress point to a much more mixed gathering than that of the Fortnightly ; in fact, women of every rank in life belong to this Club. It has five hundred members, divided into six great bodies, — the committees on reform, philanthropy, education, house-keeping, art and literature, science and philosophy. As I enter, a young blind girl, standing on the platform, is reciting a eulogy of Longfellow. It is " Poets' Day," and the meeting is devoted to the author of Evangeline. One tribute of praise follows another, with interludes of singing. After which we take up the question of the unemployed. A magistrate, who has come to discuss the matter with the Club, says that thousands of names have been registered. The University, the Theological Faculty, the Catholic Society of St. Vincent de Paul, the Salvation Army combine to remedy this distress. The ladies are asked to make visits, which are so many discreet investigations ; each of them is to call upon one of the unemployed, saying that she has heard that he has given his name to the city to be employed on street labor ; if they agree to this, she is to offer to recommend him, and, if the case be urgent, to inform the Relief-giving Society at once. I quote an excellent piece of advice offered by the judge: "Use the utmost discretion in your visits ; do not try to meddle with the affairs of the poor any more than you would do with those of · the rich." Several ladies eagerly enter upon this work with the city government. Mrs. Stevenson does not occupy her chair; it often happens that her professional duties prevent her from assisting at the meetings of the Club. Her place is on this occasion filled by a vice-president, who introduces me to various members. They show me the Club calendar for the year. I notice among the subjects which are to be discussed in different departments, from October, 1893, till June, 1894, the following titles: "Evolution of the Modern Woman ;" "Should Emigration be restricted ? " " The Meaning of Work ; " " Realism in Art and Literature ; " " Industrial Co-opera- tion ; " " Science and the Higher Life ; " " Reserve Force ; " " Co-education ;" " Maternal Rights," etc. Mrs. C. M. Sherman, well known through her philosophical works, was to write on " Dante and the Divine Vision."

I question a lady secretary in regard to the fam- ous Protective Agency ; it was established in 1886. The report of April, 1893, shows that during these

seven years seven thousand one hundred and ninety-
seven complaints of every sort have been noted,
and that $1,249,687 have been collected in small
sums. But no statistics can tell the public all
that they should know concerning a work of this
nature. Here are not only frauds and injustice
redressed, wages paid, cases of cruelty or violence
punished, guardianships assumed, divorces obtained, references investigated, illegitimate births
made regular, work found, servants placed, strangers in the city directed and helped; the poor
creatures saved by the power and mercy of this
wonderful work alone can tell what an expenditure
of sympathy, exertions, and advice the members
have lavished in behalf of their beneficiaries. This
leads us to ask whether, women being defended
with such ardor, men are not sometimes molested
in their turn. In 1889 the agency obtained the
benefit of extenuating circumstances for a woman
accused of firing in the court room upon a lawyer
who had attacked her violently. Of course the
act in itself was not approved, but the agency
proved that the wretched creature was goaded to
desperation, almost to madness, by excessive injustice and persecution. Is not the defence sometimes
a foregone conclusion? The secretary, to whom
I expressed my fears, laughed. " Oh," she replied,

" when we first take up the work, we very often have an idea that the woman is always interesting, the man always guilty ; but we soon learn to distinguish." Be this as it may, judges, police commissioners, and magistrates hold the Protective Agency in high esteem, and consider that it is of great help to them owing to its prompt and energetic action. Only those who know all the evil wrought by drunkenness and brutality in a society still as rough-hewn as that of Chicago, can understand the urgent need for this action unceasingly exercised towards women in the name of their common sisterhood, and towards all children from maternal feeling.

But the Club accomplishes many other tasks. Too often, in the United States, public offices are given for reasons which are advantageous only to politicians of the lowest order. Frightful abuses result. In certain insane asylums, the inmates, ill fed, ill clad, crowded together, slept three in a bed. The Club interfered ; and women doctors were attached to these establishments, which are now all that could be wished for. On all public boards having charge of women prisons, hospitals, and almshouses women demand a place. It is due to the Club that matrons are now attached to police stations ; it was by its suggestion that the hospital for contagious diseases was established. One of its members, Miss Sweet, started a set of ambulances, by giving the first one ; Miss Flower established a school for nurses ; Dr. Stevenson procured bath-houses for the poor on the lake and in some of the poorest districts. The Art Institute has an annual prize given by the Woman's Club. A new university was opened in 1892, to six hundred students of both sexes, with an endowment amounting to seven millions of dollars ; but the splendid structure was no sooner opened, than it was discovered that there were no dormitories for women students. The Woman's Club at once collected funds for the construction of a building which contains not only sleeping-rooms, but parlors, a large hall, a dining-room, library, and gymnasium. It was proposed to gather together homeless boys in an industrial school ; three hundred acres of land were offered on condition that buildings worth forty thousand dollars were erected ; the Woman's Club raised the money, and Glenwood School saw the light. The Club sees that the law of compulsory education is carried out; that all children from six to fourteen years of age attend school at least sixteen weeks in the year, — otherwise, many children would· stay away for want of shoes or clothes.

Lastly, the Club undertook a task more difficult than all these. It has formed a Municipal Reform League to demand that Chicago streets should be properly cleaned. If they succeed even in this, we may say that they have accomplished a miracle. A great deal has already been done; there is much less of the smoke which oppressed the city, a part of which is now consumed. In short, behind every reform we find the dauntless Woman's Club; and if they strive to reform the streets, they also wish to improve the general manners. At a meeting of the Woman's Club, some member announced that the ladies were "required" to wait for tea; a tall woman, with an air of authority, rose at the back of the hall, and sternly reproved her fellow-member, correcting her improper expression, as she called it, and demanding that she should substitute "requested" for "required."

Passengers in street cars are requested, in the name of the ladies, not to spit, and the rudest ask nothing better than to gratify their wishes. Let me give you two street incidents from Chicago. I was on the platform of a car, hesitating to plunge into the confusion of the crowded street, too timid to descend. Near me was an ill-dressed man, who looked like a vagabond, who at first seemed inclined to laugh; suddenly he sprang to the ground, helped me to the sidewalk, and when I thanked him, grunted an embarrassed "all right," and pleasantly shook me by the hand which he still held. An old German laborer (there are four hundred thousand Germans in Chicago) helped me to find my way when I was lost. As we walked along he did the honors of the city, and showed me among other things, a splendid display in a florist's window. " These are chrysanthemums," he said ; " you don't have those in France ; but [in an encouraging tone, which implied ' you may yet,'] you have the little marguerite." This somewhat contemptuous kindness is, I imagine, the exact expression of the feelings of young Chicago towards old France.

An excellent book, by Julian Ralph, "Our Great West," enumerates, to the glory of woman, all the facts relating to what he calls the "gentle side," the sweet, delicate, lofty side of Chicago. This excellent study of modern capitals in the United States, their present conditions, and their future possibilities, may be compared with another book which has recently aroused the most violent indignation, — the "Cliff Dwellers." In this study of manners, on the contrary, the bad sides, the terrible sides of Chicago are painted in very gloomy colors, — with the results of the fierce speculation, the inhuman battle for success, the merciless struggle which kills all feeling (even family feeling), hardens the soul, and leads those who yield to it to crime itself. The author of the "Cliff Dwellers," Mr. Henry Fuller, has made the more enemies by this bold satire, from the fact that he has ventured to touch the sacred personality of woman. His heroine, Cecilia Ingles, — the mundane deity, invisible until the last page, but ever present through the occult influence which she exerts, — unconsciously drives hundreds of individuals to their ruin. She only wants to produce the greatest possible effect; she does not know what her luxury costs, — how many unhappy creatures are cheated, robbed, tortured, reduced to misery, shame, and despair for her sake. Very probably this beautiful, heartless doll, placed on a pedestal of dollars, exists in Chicago, — at least, many such instances may have been born there, — but I imagine she did not stay there. We should expect rather to find her in Europe, where she is in pursuit of a title, and proposes, as her last caprice, to force her way, by dint of money, either into the Faubourg St. Germain, or — preferably, for she prizes difficulties and scorns republics — into the most inaccessible ranks of the English aristocracy. Let us add that in either direction she succeeds admirably, which insures her a long train of imitators; and in her new country no one laughs more loudly than she at Chicago, the Woman's Club, and all the rest.

PRIVATE HOUSES IN CHICAGO. — STREETS AND HOMES. — THE TEMPLE.

To laugh at Chicago is a bad habit common to all civilized America. The shrill, nasal voice of its citizens; their trivial manners; the big feet of its women; the enormity of bad taste shown in its tall buildings, its "sky scrapers;" the almost fabulous growth of that huge mushroom, or rather of that wild onion (if we are to believe in the Indian etymology of *Checagua*), — all come in for their share of criticism. But say what we will, onion or cryptogam, it is a marvellous growth. It is the best evidence of the power and the industry of a great nation. Is not the resurrection of that city, a miracle indeed, — that city which, scarcely sixty years old, perished almost wholly in the fire of 1870, but sprang up from its ashes a thousand times richer and more active, its prosperity increasing even while we gaze?

Would-be jokers still quote the dialogue between a native of St. Louis and a citizen of Chicago who were quarrelling over the merits of their respective cities: —

"When were you in Chicago?"

"Last week."

"Oh, well! Then you know nothing about it. The city has been entirely changed since then."

But the witticism is stale; it is no longer possible to compare Chicago with St. Louis, which has been left far behind; to the passing stranger one represents a great provincial town, the other a capital.

With no wish to offend certain Eastern exquisites who went most reluctantly to the World's Fair, and who, once there, looked at nothing save the "white city," refusing to set foot in the "black city," I must confess that I saw nothing at the Chicago exhibition so curious as Chicago itself. I felt the fascination of the monster as soon as it appeared to me from the railroad, rising from the midst of the vast plain, where, preceded by the city of workmen, — Pullman, an annex worthy of it, — it lies stretched along the shore of its lake, beneath a canopy of smoke. Its boisterous energy impressed me from the very first day, and its architecture amazed me. Not

that I have any great admiration for the buildings, all height and no width, which rival the
Eiffel tower; but there are excellent specimens
of the architecture to which Richardson gave his
name, — a composite and yet original architecture, a mixture of Roman, Byzantine, and a little
Gothic very happily applied to modern wants, to
great stores and industrial establishments. Marshall Field's vast warehouse, for instance, is a
masterpiece of this kind. In its place and of
its kind it does as much honor to Richardson as
the famous Trinity Church at Boston, expressing
equally well the purpose to which it is devoted;
what has been called the severity of its aspect
does not exclude beauty, a solid, massive, im-
perishable beauty, as the cyclopean appearance
of its rough-hewn, rock-faced walls seems to
proclaim.

The new American architecture, which has
ceased to have anything in common with colonial
architecture with its formal lines, reminding us
of Louis XVI. and the Empire, — that architecture which strikes us as the most marked
manifestation of the progress of the fine arts
in America, — has also been very successfully '
adapted to the requirements of domestic life.
In this form it flourishes particularly in the

northern part of the city. The tree-planted
streets leading to the lake are lined with dwellings which, when they are not pretentious and
odd, are charming. There is a medley of all
styles, which yet resembles nothing known, —
a compromise between the castle and the cottage,
an ingenious confusion where discords sometimes
result in harmony. As we look at those picturesquely irregular porches, those turreted gables,
those piazzas filled with flowers, we feel that if
the inmate is like his shell, the people of the
West have been slandered: they have at least
imagination. We cross the threshold: good
pictures cover the walls, even in houses which
do not contain important collections; everywhere
we see antique tapestries and valuable furniture.
Let us draw no hasty conclusions from this. No
doubt most of the fortunate owners of these
things still depend on the taste of their archi-
tect; but still their education is assuredly pro-
gressing, — they are learning to know what is
beautiful by possessing it. Their wives, too,
do much to enlighten them. Many rich men
have married away from Chicago; as the Romans
carried off the Sabines. The mistress of a superb
mansion on Prairie Avenue said, as she invited
me to a luncheon and named over the ladies who

were to be present, — " Not one of them is from
Chicago, although they all belong to its top
crust." Shall I venture to say that three or
four of the most agreeable of those whom I met
elsewhere were merely natives? Yes, indeed, we
find all sorts and kinds in Chicago, — noisy up-
starts of vulgar aspect, and women as distinguished
in face, dress, and mind as if they had been born
in the East; æsthetic interiors where art and
literature are discussed, and factories like for-
tresses elbowing other granite mountains, which
every day, about six o'clock, vomit forth thousands of business men into the dirtiest streets in
the world; palaces of millionnaires, and piles of
offices where you drop from the fourteenth or
even the twentieth floor, stunned by the dizzy
speed of the elevator; superb parks and vast
pieces of waste land; caravansaries with onyx
walls and mosaic pavements like the Auditorium
(which also contains a magnificent theatre), and
oyster palaces, public houses, breweries, wine-
rooms and beer saloons, suited to every taste,
even the basest. There are butcheries of cattle
which put all slaughter-houses to shame; stock-
yards where lovers of carnage may see the blood
of pigs flow in torrents; and there are great
butchers who are also the greatest of all phil-

anthropists. There is Armour Institute, that model school of arts and trades to which its founder gave $1,400,000, not to mention the mission of the same name where there are a library, a kindergarten, a dispensary, and where every Sunday eighteen hundred young men and women, many of whom would otherwise be homeless, meet to learn the meaning of spiritual life, intellectual life, family life, and honest amusement. Mr. Armour spends the afternoon with his children, those whom he pleasantly calls "his partners." And here too, behind this colossal humanitarian scheme, as behind the industrial schemes which feed it, there is, it seems, feminine collaboration.

When I was shown a splendid structure thirteen stories high, only eight less than the Masonic Temple, with the words, "That is the Woman's Temple," I was not at all surprised; it seemed quite natural that this public symbol of veneration and gratitude should be reared in the principal street of the business quarter, amid the confusion of the Exchange, the Chamber of Commerce, Insurance Companies, etc. I was then told that the Temple, so called for short, is that of temperance, that it was erected by women. Its construction cost more than a million dollars, and it was a woman who provided the funds; a woman who possesses that talent which is most rare among her sex, — the financial talent. Mrs. M. B. Carse spent ten years in the realization of her plan, and succeeded in carrying it out with the aid of another woman famous for the aid which she has lent for twenty years past to the Temperance Union, — Miss Willard. Frances Willard has devoted her life to preaching the system of self-government; she is at the head of the White Cross movement, which, in many States, has obtained the passage of special laws for the protection of woman. The avowed antagonist of America's mortal foe, drunkenness, she attacks it with every weapon upon which she can lay her hand. The Temperance Society wraps all cities, big and little, in its busy net-work; she has chosen her headquarters in the city where this evil flourishes most fearfully, and it seems that philanthropy is, as it should ever be, according to American ideas, at the same time a good thing from a business point of view, since the annual income from the Temple buildings is supposed to amount to $50,000.

Members of the Temperance Society are bound by an oath which condemns them to the most insipid drinks. In their homes you are offered nothing but ice-water, ginger ale, or at most unfermented grape-juice, which tastes like fruit-syrup. I remember the contemptuous glances cast at me in hotels or restaurants by certain ladies who saw me drinking wine. I was evidently a subject for scandal, — a thing to be avoided at any cost in America. The following anecdote was told me by a friend, who did not hesitate to offer me claret and even champagne at luncheon: An Italian lady, visiting Chicago, was invited to a house where temperance ran riot. "What will you take to drink?" asked the hostess, "tea, coffee, or cocoa?" The stranger innocently answered that she usually drank wine. "Very good, only you must let us serve it to you in a teapot, so that no one may be shocked."

The Foreign Population of Chicago. — Hull House.

In speaking of the Temperance Temple, I am sorry not to allude to other great buildings of Chicago; but the list would be too long, to say nothing of the fact that it lies outside my subject. Those giants, whose heights have lately been limited by law to one hundred and fifty feet, are still multiplied, and it is most curious to watch their rapid construction. The bare steel frame is first erected, and then clothed with brick or stone, as with a more or less beautiful garment. The masons often begin the casing at the upper stories, which may already be occupied, while the foundations of the structure seem scarcely yet in position. An elevator takes you to the eighth floor in a store where everything is sold, — from clothes to food, from silverware to kitchen utensils, — while the ground floor is still unfinished and open to the weather. The sidewalk made of glass tiles affords the basement ample light; as for the cellar, the soft clay in which the foundation is dug does not permit of such a thing. It would take a Turner and a Raphael combined to reproduce the effect of the crowded streets of Chicago, of those "sky scrapers," illuminated at night by an intermittent electric light. Blazing bunches of every color are fastened here and there by way of advertisement and placard; other advertisements are hung from house to house across the broad street, which is filled with a dull roar like the voice of the sea, the constant strokes of a gong announcing the uninterrupted passage of electric or cable cars. And through this steady uproar, with no loud outcry, without confusion or disorder, flows a human flood wherein you recognize specimens from the whole world over. Out of the one million one hundred thousand inhabitants of Chicago, there are not actually more than three hundred thousand native Americans. Germans, Irish, Swedes, and Poles elbow and push, all apparently in the utmost haste, no one moving out of a straight course lest he overthrow his neighbor. Here and there a tiny fruit-stand crowded into the corner of a well-smoked wall reminds you of Italy, with its garlands of grapes and bananas, its pyramids of lemons, oranges, and red apples, and its Californian fruit more tempting to the eye than to the taste. Two black eyes gleam in this poor but cheerful frame, — the fiery eyes of a Sicilian, who lounges behind the wares which he knows so well how to show to the best advantage; for lazy and undisciplined as he may seem, he has a sense of the picturesque.

Here is a great display of the negro race, which swarms, often worse than ragged, but always smiling; also fair, placid Scandinavian faces; Bohemians, in such numbers that Chicago is the third Bohemian city; Israelitish types, with swarthy skin and hooked noses, — like the Jew, who, standing at the entrance to the panorama of Jerusalem, does the honors of Doré's picture and sells you water from the Jordan.

I had an opportunity to study this motley crowd of every type and every tint at the funeral rites of Mayor Harrison, murdered on the eve of his marriage, by one of those lunatics, those cranks, who are hung without hesitation in America precisely as if they were sane, so soon as they take it into their heads to disturb law and order. Harrison was a politician of much popularity among the lovers of that sort of liberty which consists in keeping bars, theatres, and gambling houses open on Sunday. A sympathetic mob accordingly flocked to his obsequies. I never saw so many evil faces. The procession was very late in appearing on the road which leads from the church to the cemetery. The Chicago police-men — colossal men, who seem made expressly to hold a population of criminals in awe — drove the curious spectators roughly back on either side of the street, without arousing complaint. Ab-solute silence reigned; no sign of impatience during the interminable wait, no remark when the funeral procession at last appeared, — a pro-cession which continued two hours to the sound of military music. Militia, clubs, freemasons with their regalia, official characters delegated

from the various districts of the city, followed
the hearse, which was in strangely bad taste, —
all on horseback or in carriages, hat on head as a
matter of course, and galloping towards the distant cemetery.   No time is lost in burying the
dead in a land which is pre-eminently the land of
the living.   It was the first of November, — as it
were a final scene in the World's Fair, the closing scene.   In every buttonhole gleamed the portrait of Harrison, painted in silver on a black
rosette; but I saw no other sign of emotion.   The
interesting side of the spectacle was the crowd,
in which Russian Jews furnished a pitiful con-
tingent.   Emigration, involuntary emigration, has
cast this flood upon the shores of the New World,
most unfortunately, — a flood of people ignorant
of the language, ignorant of the law, and forming
with the worst of the Italians a justifiable source
of alarm to the country which has received them.
Their misery seems to be without a remedy, because it is the result not only of every misfortune, but of every vice, of every form of revolt,
and of utter incapacity.   Exiles in a new world,
where every man works for himself with unheard-
of vigor, persistence, and perseverance, there
could scarcely be any alternative for them than to
fall a prey to the gallows or to die of hunger, were

it not for the tireless compassion of women which assures to them bread and creates work for them.

Hull House is among other things the refuge of poor foreigners. Hull House was founded by Miss Jane Addams. We are told that she took her inspiration from one of the best philanthropic institutions in England, — Toynbee Hall. We are also told that there are hundreds of houses much like hers in the United States, and indeed there is scarcely a city where I did not find well-organized settlements. But that of Miss Addams still stands alone, owing to the character lent it by the personality of its head, and to the match-less influence which she exerts.

The theory that the rich need the poor as much as the poor need the rich lay at the root of all the plans formed by Miss Addams; she devoted her fortune, her time, and her intellect to the service of this idea. To begin with, she bought a dilapidated estate in a wretched quarter of the town. It had been used for auctions, and was known as Hull House from the name of its builder. She repaired it, improved it; gave it a clean, bright, homelike aspect; then established herself there with her friend and partner, Miss Starr. Many others came by degrees to play a greater or less part in the work.

The simplest way to let my reader know what goes on at Hull House is to ask him to go there with me.

With the person who was to introduce me, I jolted one evening for a long distance in a carriage over an atrocious pavement, through muddy streets, lined with miserable hovels and those saloons which are both gambling hells and bars. At last we stop before a large building, with brightly lighted windows. At the door I am greeted by a lively, smiling young woman, Miss Ellen Starr. To her I owe my first view of the establishment, which she shows me from cellar to garret. The hour is a favorable one, for all the members of "Jane's Club" have come in. This club of working-girls, placed as it were under the tutelary care of Miss Addams, forms an independent annex of Hull House, of which it is at the same time one of the most interesting features. The young girls belonging to it all earn their living as dressmakers, milliners, seamstresses, shop-girls, stenographers, printers, typewriters, etc. Formerly dispersed among various boarding-houses and more or less respectable lodging-houses, they have here the shelter of a home where their habits are refined by daily associations. A very clever German woman has charge of the club's money matters, it being now self-supporting. In the parlor I find two young girls taking a music lesson, their day's work being over; another, just returned from her shop, is finishing a late supper in the pleasant dining-room, lighted like all the rest of the house by gas, and warmed by a furnace, — a customary luxury in America, and one which is generally carried too far, for almost everywhere the heat is stifling. Many of the girls have gone to their rooms on the second and third floor. Miss Starr asks leave to show their dominions to a foreign lady passing through Chicago, and they consent with the good grace of those who know that they have nothing to lose by being viewed at close quarters. Indeed, the rooms are almost elegant, — rooms with two, three, and four beds mostly, but divided by screens and curtains, and having at the first glance a look of order and perfect neatness. Some girls are resting, read-ing, in rocking-chairs; others are beginning to undress, or are combing their hair before the glass. Taking them thus by surprise, I have an immediate proof of Miss Starr's words: "They become more refined every day," — refined by daily contact with all that is best in woman. I apologize for my intrusion, and they reply with

a courtesy which would amaze me had I not had
time to make acquaintance in America with
others of the same rank under different circumstances. To be sure, they have profited by all
the advantages offered by Hull House, — books,
lectures, etc. Miss Starr is giving them a special
course on art, and tells me that her pupils often
bring her their scanty savings to be used in buy-
ing photographs, which are sent them from Italy,
— photographs from the works of the old masters, which I actually saw on the walls of the
house. The preference of a large majority is for
Botticelli. Botticelli popular in the suburbs of
Chicago, — is not that strange? It is, I suppose,
largely due to the influence of Miss Starr's teachings, and also to the influence of the physical
type of Miss Addams, who looks singularly like a
Botticelli with her saintly face, pale, anxious,
with slightly hollow cheeks, pensive brow, great
deep eyes whose gaze seems but half conscious
of all save pain and misery. "I do not mean,"
explains Miss Starr, "that all our girls have such
delicate tastes. There are some who love dress
and frivolity; they too are free to follow their
bent. To lead them higher we count upon the
example of others, and upon the atmosphere of the
house, where the life is in no way austere. Every

week they give a little party: music, refresh-
ments — nothing is wanting. They have their
share of honest superfluity." Miss Starr's kind
face shines at the thought.

We return to the main building. A wide passage-way divides it into two parts; on either
hand there are large rooms, which I enter to see
what goes on every night. In the first study room
a Canadian lady is teaching French to a dozen
scholars; in the second a reading is going on; in
another some young people are drawing, girls and
men working together.

Sons of the rich men of Chicago take charge
of the Boys' Club, entering into friendly relations
with these once outcast lads, who now learn all
sorts of things as if for amusement, — modelling,
wood-carving, geography, American history, even
a little Latin, to say nothing of all sorts of games
suited to their age. They have a splendid gymnasium lighted up as if it were day, where I saw
them exercising; after which some took a shower
bath. The baths established at Hull House have
contributed as much as anything else towards the
moral and physical health of the region. But
the great benefit is the kitchen. At meal time
a good and substantial bill of fare awaits all who
wish to be fed at the lowest possible price.

Some carry home a dish, and lessons may be learned which are as valuable as many others; for there is a school specially managed by young ladies in that bright, attractive kitchen furnished with all the newest and most economical arrangements. Ladies also are faithful attendants at the sewing-classes, where little girls hear stories while they work, which keep their imagination active. Some also help in the kindergarten, which meets every morning in the big room at other times known as the play-room of the neighborhood children. No one is forgotten, great or small, old or young. Miss Addams desires the poor foreigners who live in the neighborhood to retain all that is good of their respective lands; therefore, each nationality has its club. One of the most successful is the Friday Evening German Club, where old popular songs are sung, and Schiller is read, while knitting-needles move apace.

We pass rapidly through reading-rooms filled with laborers looking over the newspapers and magazines of all countries. Upstairs, we find a billiard table and various amusements. "Very often," says Miss Starr, "it is a desire for sociability which leads the weakest to frequent drinking and gambling dens. We do not wish our

men to have that excuse. To be sure, many are
not content with what we offer; but few as we
may bring in, they are so many saved. Besides,
they can come every night to one of the clubs
which I have showed you, — the. German club,
the gymnastic club, the drawing club, or the
political economy club. We are very proud of
our picture gallery, where we have already had
five exhibitions. Picture owners are very generous in lending us their treasures."

The idea of alms, as we see, is wholly absent
from the system of Miss Addams. She eases the
life of the poor; that is all. She puts into it as
much as possible of the things whose possession they envy the rich; or, rather, she tries to
efface distinctions by establishing neighborly relations between rich and poor, — "men, women,
and children," as she says, "joining in one
family, as God meant them to be." She asks no
one concerning his creed. The general belief is
Christian humanitarianism, the spirit of Christ
shown in works of love.

Help comes to her from every hand. Let me
tell you the story of the great play-ground, where
children have ample room to play the athletic
games which seem to be a part of American institutions. A horrible tenement house once stood

there, — a filthy hive, where poor laborers lived, huddled together, under the worst possible conditions for health, and in the most objectionable promiscuity. The owner of this building, which Miss Addams thought the worst in her whole neighborhood, lived abroad, and paid little heed to the way in which his property was managed. But Miss Addams having complained of the condition of things, he at once atoned for his unconscious errors, ordered the buildings torn down, and offered Hull House the land. The boys of the neighborhood now have a splendid play-ground, which the city, not wishing to be under too great a burden of obligation, has put under the charge of a special policeman.

When, at a late hour, we leave that house of refuge and help which shines through the night like a beacon of safety, the door of our carriage is opened by a passing lad. " A, few years ago that boy and his mates would have thrown stones at us," says the friend accompanying me.

My most interesting visit to Hull House was on an evening when the Workingmen's Club met, — a club where social science gladly uses the language of anarchy. I was invited to dinner. Miss Addams, at the head of the long table, carves and talks, as any hostess might do. On the walls of

the large room, whose furniture shines with neatness, hang big carbon photographs, reproductions
of Millet's most famous pictures and some masterpieces of Italian art. The whitest of table-cloths,
simple but abundant fare; nothing but water to
drink, of course, — temperance reigns supreme.
My right-hand neighbor, who has studied law in
Paris, talks of his student life; like most of the
guests, he is one of the helpers of Miss Addams,
temporary or permanent inmates of Hull House.
Among them, I recognize with some surprise two
young lawyers with whom I dined the week before
in very different company. Bachelors are allowed
to invite and receive ladies on certain fixed days,
at their respective clubs. I was therefore invited to
a very literary and very agreeable dinner, washed
down by excellent champagne, at one of the great
Chicago clubs. Wholly absorbed in worldly matters on that occasion, my two friends hardly seemed
like reformers devoted to philanthropic work. I
inquire, and learn that such instances are not rare.
Every one brings what he can to this charitable
league, — merchants, doctors, teachers, professors,
students, clergymen, and mothers who are glad to
give at least a few moments to the day nursery
which helps so many other mothers. These gentlemen tell me simply that they have engaged board

at Hull House for three or four weeks. They
speak without the least pride of the work which
they are doing, and which is anything but easy,
— to inspire confidence in the embittered or mis-
trustful, to study their wants, to help them to help
themselves. Evidently they would be amazed,
they would be embarrassed, if any admiration
were expressed for that which seems to them
only natural.

After dinner we go into the parlor, where for
nearly half an hour the conversation turns upon
the most varied subjects, — travels, fine arts, etc.
I talk with a book-lover who knows all our fine edi-
tions and orders his bindings from Paris. Much
is said concerning France. Here, as elsewhere, I
feel that France does not hold the first place.
They admit that the French have discovered, in-
vented, inaugurated everything, but feel that we
have been surpassed by broader intellects and more
steady purposes. Great sympathy is expressed
for France, but there is not so much esteem
in the opinions which are pronounced with the
utmost politeness. We are measured according to
the revelations of our novelists, who are ranked
very high from a purely literary point of view,
although there is a pretence that only those of
their works are read which are least harmful to

morals. "André Cornelis," "Cosmopolis," and
the psychological essays of Paul Bourget are
praised ; also a series of tales by Maupassant, said
to be admirably translated by Bunner, who himself
excels in short stories. Pierre Loti is also known
through translations, — to which I impatiently reply
that in that case he is not known at all. This remark is scarcely understood; for manner is far
less important than matter in America, even in
the eyes of those who call themselves artists. But
Alphonse Daudet meets with universal favor.
"Sappho" is classed not only among clever but
among good books.

A muffled sound of footsteps and of voices has
for some time been heard in the hall. Eight
o'clock strikes; we all return to the dining-room,
which has been changed to a lecture room. A
drawn curtain reveals a platform, and in front of
it, benches and chairs are already well filled. The
prevailing element is cosmopolitan : plenty of those
Russian Jews whom I have met before, thin,
bearded, with prominent cheek-bones; their black
eyes, sad unto desolation or burning like those of
hungry wolves, speak of long persecutions, weary
wanderings, hopeless exile. Do they understand
English ? Few of them, I fancy; the others, with
one elbow on their knee, their chin in one hand,

78

eagerly stretch their necks as if to grasp some help
from a word.   But at first it seems as if the speaker
could not utter any words of consolation.   He is
a professor from the University, — a Baptist minister too, — tall, cold, and intelligent, very correct
in his white collar and long frock coat.   Before
he begins to speak, the president chosen for the
evening, a little old man from the neighborhood,
seated on the platform by a table, upon which lies
Miss Addams's watch like a call to order, — the
president says in a jocose tone, addressing the
audience: " We are told that we have with us
to-night a person of great learning, a famous professor.   No doubt he will instruct and at the same
time amuse us."   The satire is appreciated by
many.   Bitter or ominous smiles cross more than
one face, then profound silence ensues.

   This death-like silence lasts, without the shadow
of an interruption, for an hour, — the allotted time,
— while Mr. H. discusses the social problems,
which are universally thrust upon the attention of
the world, trying to prove that it is wrong to make
individuals responsible for changes caused by the
advance of trade.   He declares himself to be moved
with pity for the errors of anarchy, which he under-
stands and excuses, but which society cannot toler-
ate ; he asks of the laborer patience, steady effort,

the economy so seldom practised in America,
just as he asks of the rich, in order somewhat to
equalize matters, generous sacrifices which can only
be voluntary. All that he says is very wise; but
we feel, he himself must feel, that there is no current of sympathy between his audience and himself. Some of the men scribble on bits of paper.

When he stops, the little old president, whose
wrinkled face reminds us of Voltaire, winks his
red eyes mischievously, and says in the same in-
cisive tone, which makes him very funny: " I pro-
phesied that you would instruct and amuse us.
You have certainly amused us." Then he gives
the floor for six minutes to one of the foreigners, —
a Bohemian, I think, — who rises trembling with
emotion, pale to the very lips. His jargon is at
first scarcely intelligible, but what he says is in
no way ordinary, and by force of will, he makes
himself understood. "It may be," he declares,
" apparently no one is guilty, therefore we bear no
grudge to any one; but what are we to do? I
was a shoemaker; suppose I offer now to make a
shoe, myself alone, when there are machines for
nailing and sewing all the separate parts! The
man who has learned a trade and can no longer
support himself by it, is dismissed without any
compensation. Moreover, you are right, — there

is no vengeance to be taken for all this; we can only wait. Nature takes it upon herself to suppress all that is useless or bad. When you see a drunkard reeling across the street, you know that it will not last long, that his degraded existence will soon be ended through the very fault of him who leads it. Well! when I see a useless man roll by me in his carriage, I feel that the same holds good for him and his like. Wait!"

I am sure that I have added nothing to the words of this singular creature, who certainly must have read Schopenhauer; indeed, I took notes. His bony hand, clutching the back of the chair before him, trembled constantly while he struggled with the difficulties of a peculiar accent, impossible to describe. His face was a fine one, marked and brown like that of an Arab. When he had done, he closed his eyes and stood quivering, his chin resting on his heaving chest.

After him a big, pale fellow, with an amiable expression, asked a few questions, apparently in good faith, as to the means of finding work; he had not succeeded either by help of the churches or through the charitable associations. Another, as sunburned as any present, but with the red of whiskey in his cheeks, declared, almost with a laugh, that for his part he did not object to steam

saws, knowing how hard it was to use his arms,
in all sorts of weather, in thick forests, and for
years at a time. To say nothing of the fact that
in the three years when he had worked hardest,
he had only earned enough for his food and lodging. Was that fair?

Then a little German rose, furious as a dog about
to bite; he had the face of a pug, with a turned-
up nose, big prominent eyes, yellow bristles, a
nasal and vibrating voice: "It is all very well
for professors and ministers, it is all very well for
loafers," he exclaimed, "to instruct those who are
killing themselves with work. They have no right
to do so unless they come and live among us, and
work hard with us. They know very well that
society is ill organized, and that in justice everything ought to be changed from beginning to end,
willy nilly; but they will not admit it for fear they
should lose their places and their salaries, poltroons,
cowards, and thieves that they are."

The irascible German spent more than the allotted
six minutes in invectives which the cunning president reluctantly cut short. The professor showed
much patience. He listened, without a word of
answer, to the insults hurled at him. I am amazed
that Miss Addams allows her guests to be so ill-
treated. Miss Starr bends anxiously to her ear,

and seems to beg her to interfere; but I seem to hear her reply: "We know them; they are not so terrible as they seem." She therefore maintains an impartial attitude, it being her conviction that all this rage and rancor require a safety valve. Besides, mental labor is to find defenders.

A delicate young man, with light-blue Irish eyes, better dressed than the others, a watch-chain across his waistcoat, protests against the term "loafers" applied to all who are not mere day-laborers. He has, he says, worked in both ways, and he feels that brain work is the hardest work of all. He tells his own experiences in very simple style. After years of utter destitution, he went to California and had charge of a large ranch, with many men under him. Of these men some prosper, as he has prospered. But to succeed, more is required of a man than merely to do his duty; that is not enough in an age of mad competition. Then he quotes the case of two boys, his subordinates. One was a good worker in so far as he did his work to the letter; he was paid and dismissed when his task was ended. The other worked night and day, defying all rivalry by his zeal; he now earns seventy dollars a month. The speaker's conclusion was that to succeed a man must have the will to succeed, — not a mere weak will, which so many have, but *real* will : a gesture completed his thought. No doubt this fair-haired fellow, with muscles of steel, desired success, — desired it until there was no flesh left on his bones.

Several others also spoke; many of them were foolish and clumsy: theirs were but the vague stammerings of anarchy. Finally, the little, bent, wrinkled president, with his bristling white hair, made a show of passion. He too would reply to the grand professor who recommends economy to those who have nothing, work to those who are driven away from every shop; and who showed himself so hard on tramps, or vagabonds, seeming to confound them with criminals. " A vagabond! Why, Jesus Christ was nothing more! The gospel says: ' Foxes have holes and birds have nests, but the Son of Man hath not where to lay his head? ' If Christ were to return, his ministers, far from acknowledging him, would hand him over to the police to be locked up. Savings indeed! One would think a man had nothing to do but to go to the bank and deposit his little hoard. Christ did not save; he had no home. And this is the way the false apostles of the present day, who are supposed to teach his doctrine, talk! "

The little president paces the platform, shrugging his shoulders, his hands in his pockets. But Miss

Addams's watch, on which he keeps his eye, warns
him to stop; and then the event proves that the
patron saint of the place was right in her favorite
theory.

It seems as if the insults lavished upon him like
hail had struck a spark from that somewhat rigid
scholar, who came hither resting on his honorable
superiority. He was accused in the name of the
gospel, — in the gospel, in his turn, he finds a
defensive weapon; but he uses it humorously, in
a familiar way, which will change the feeling of
the club towards him. Straightening his herculean
form, he says: "If I have spoken ill of vagabonds, it strikes me that you have treated me as
a coward, a loafer, and a thief; I think we are
quits. I see but one way to carry on a conversation started on this plane, — to go out into the
street with you, and have it out with you with blows ;
but there, too, you might be too strong for me. I
prefer to admit that there is truth in much that
you have said ; but insults never amount to anything, especially when we fling them at strangers.
I might tell you the story of my life, show you
how hard it has been; but what would be the use?
I will only tell you this: My father was both doctor and clergyman, and was a credit to both professions. It can no longer be so; a doctor now

has all he can do to keep up with the advance of
science, — he must become a specialist, choose between the various branches. The same man can
no longer manufacture, as you just now said, even
a shoe by himself alone. To win any sort of a
position now requires much greater persistence
than it once did; a man must concentrate his attention on a single object. So I, for myself, would be
glad to work with my hands for my own pleasure;
and, strong as I am, it would do me good to turn
over the soil in a garden for two or three hours
a day. But I cannot do this, because you trust
your children to me to educate, and you naturally
expect me to be wholly absorbed in my task, which
is to instruct them. My friends, many things are
put into the mouths of the ministers of religion,
forgetting that these opinions are almost all repeated by a special class of individuals, — those
who never go to church. It is these people who
charge us with ignorance of Christ. Perhaps I
spoke too severely of vagabonds, who do nothing
worse than to secure food and lodging; they too
are my brothers. But having several brothers,
you will allow that it is admissible to have a preference for one or the other of them, — for the
one who leads the most straightforward life, and
gives the least trouble, although we may be

ready all the same to lend a hand to the others, not forgetting to punish them if necessary. I know that kind of love. I·was the only boy in a large family, and I had plenty of love; but it did n't prevent me from catching all the licking."

At the word "licking" there was some laughter, followed by applause. Then, emboldened by his expression of good-will for even the worst, a few men offered their hands to Mr. H., who had at last struck the right key. I am astonished to see the fiery German among them. He stands for some time in a door-way talking and arguing with the victim of his insolent outburst, who, like a good Christian, seems to have forgotten all the names bestowed on him.

The meeting breaks up after a few words from Miss Starr, announcing the next meeting, and the fact that a famous preacher would speak of religious matters with all who were interested. They would be allowed to express their doubts and personal ideas in writing; but she hoped, for the honor of the house, that they would be good enough to remember the respect due to guests who came there as friends and with the best of motives. She ingeniously addresses a few indirect reproaches to the men, who receive them with half timid, half indifferent manner.

But Miss Addams is surrounded by a group to whom she explains that a great stock of coal having been laid in for Hull House, they can come there and buy it cheaper than at retail. The news is welcome at the beginning of winter; but I fancy that those poor wretches are more benefited still by the kindness of the look which she fixes on them, — a look full of suffering, for Miss Addams's eyes, beautiful as they are, have just undergone a painful operation. This has no more effect than anything else in turning her from her customary task. Delicate from her early youth, she has answered the medical decree that she could only live if spared all fatigue, by an extraordinary expenditure of energy. And she lives as by a miracle: she forgets her body; she is possibly the most perfect and unconscious instance of the kind of moral hygiene now popular in the United States under the name of Christian Science, of which I shall take occasion to speak later.

As a matter of course, Miss Addams is a member of the Woman's Club like Mrs. Carse, like Miss Willard, like Mrs. Logan, whom charity has led to the most repulsive of all duties, that of the police. Mrs. Logan is the chief matron, and does an incalculable amount of good in that posi-

tion.   Criminals and unfortunates are indiscriminately conducted to one and the same station;
there she subjects them to a sifting process.   She
takes care of such poor girls as have still a linger-
ing spark of moral sense, and insures them the
means to rise.   She pleads for her protégées, if
need be, goes with them to the judge to give
them courage, knows no fatigue or disgust.

Such women should surely be allowed the right
to demand certain privileges, for they undertake
tremendous tasks.   I am made acquainted with
their work by one of the celebrities of Chicago,
— Mrs. Margaret Sullivan, a brilliant journalist,
who daily writes the leading article in the
"Herald."   She says: "The power of American
women reformers lies in the fact that they have
always personally deserved public esteem; not
one of them has dipped into eccentricities of base
quality, such as advocating free love, or making
a parade of dangerous socialist theories.   Even
the earliest in date, those who put themselves
forward with more noise than is common now,
and who drew down upon themselves the sort of
ridicule which affects shriekers, were, without
exception, irreproachable from the point of view
of morals.   The Stantons, the Anthonys, the
Lucy Stones, those apostles of the emancipation

of woman, may have been berated as fanatics and ranters at first, but they were always respected as honest women. The most advanced members of the Woman's Club are good wives and mothers. Accordingly, the men see no reason for opposing the movement which they lead; they applaud their efforts and their triumphs. Whenever it shall please women to claim complete political rights, the men of their family and their circle will not resist; they are restrained by their own wisdom."

Mrs. Sullivan said this as she showed me the offices, the presses, and the entire, vast, and magnificent establishment of the "Herald." No writer on its staff receives a higher salary than she, which is saying a great deal. Three other women are regularly employed on this paper. I take great pleasure in talking with one of them, Mrs. Mary Abbott, who has charge of the purely literary part, — book notices, book news, etc. We see that women are everywhere to the fore in Chicago. Probably no name of all the names of those who organized the World's Fair was repeated so often as that of Mrs. Potter Palmer; and a young girl, a graceful poet, with the face of a muse, — Miss Harriet Monroe, — was commissioned to write the Columbian ode recited on the four hundredth anniversary of the discovery

of America, October 21, 1892, during the inaug-
ural festival of the Palace of Liberal Arts. Certain passages, set to music, were given by a
chorus of five thousand voices, accompanied by
a vast orchestra and brass bands. Miss Monroe,
who belongs to a family of artists and writers,
is the author of a tragedy in verse and of short
poems by no means to be regarded as Western
wild weeds. Lovers of that class of products
must seek them in the very variegated garden of
Eugene Field, pre-eminently the local writer.

I have said that Chicago combines all sorts of
contrasts; but nothing is more unexpected than
the dominion of woman in that great centre of
vigorous manhood, in that focus of traffic and
trade, where everything at first sight seems rough,
the climate and the ambient atmosphere, both
moral and physical. Nowhere did it seem to me so
strongly marked; although from North to South,
and from East to West, to sum up my impressions, I heard but a paraphrase of John Stuart
Mill's assertion, so eloquently commented upon
by Mrs. Maud Howe Elliott, in speaking of the
World's Fair: "Woman's hour has struck." It
has indeed struck in the United States, with the
chivalric consent of man.

II.

BOSTON.

I SPENT more time in Boston than in any other city of the Union; and the longer I lived there, the fonder I became of it. But this required no great effort, — the first impression was enough; and even now, when I try to recall my memories, the thought of Boston is all predominant! Before it dawned upon me as the most polished city in America, Boston dazzled me as a dream of beauty. This may perhaps be due to the circumstances of my arrival. It was evening; and next morning, when I woke, I saw from my window, the blinds being open, a panorama which I can never forget. Beneath a cloudless sky, deeply tinged with rose, — one of those American skies which seem so much loftier than those of France, — stretched the wonderful Charles River, sparkling as if sprinkled with diamonds, broad as an arm of the sea. No passing steamer disturbed its solitude at that early hour; it was not the season when it is covered with pleasure boats; not a sloop, or a schooner on the horizon, — only a dredging-machine cast its black shadow on

that sun-flecked sheet. The water, which is subject to the influence of the tide, flowed up to the
wall of the garden beneath my window, washing
on one side the semicircular quay bordered by
straight, red, lofty roofs and on the other, one
of the Cambridge bridges. Opposite, beyond
the long bridge, flung boldly between the two
sister cities which are in constant communication, wooded hills were outlined in the atmosphere of crystalline purity. The factories and
warehouses built on piles, to my right, looked
like great monuments with their square towers,
their massive silhouettes. The telegraph poles,
whose quivering shadows were reflected in the
water, — sea, stream, great canal or lagoon, —
seemed waiting for some one to moor up a fleet
of gondolas to them. I could almost fancy myself in Venice; and the peaceful aspect of the
scene completed the illusion. But Charles
River sunrises are as nothing compared to the
sunsets. I remember, in winter, certain opaline
thaws, — the sky becoming a vivid red towards
four o'clock, then gradually brightening and passing through every shade of orange and greenish
yellow, into the clearest blue, the calm and
almost somnolent water serving as a mirror for
this magic show. Still frozen along the shore,

its cakes of ice glimmered in the light of the earliest street lamps. I remember too, in seasons of remorseless cold, the aurora-borealis-like tones of sky and water, — houses, boats and naked trees standing out against that crimson in black relief whose slightest details were most clearly marked; then the conflagration, growing smoky, died out by degrees, leaving ashes only, after the disappearance of a large red rayless ball, the strange Northern sun. The wavy line of the hills faded into that expiring gray. And twilight once fallen, the Charles River looked like a lake of quivering steel, in which the lines of fire lighted along the wharves and on the long bridge were extended into infinity; as each car passed, invisible in the darkness, showers of sparks lit up all the windows in the great buildings on the Cambridge shore, which in this intermittent illumination more than ever assumed the aspect of fairy palaces, commonplace though they might actually be.

The very variable climate, with its sudden changes from one extreme to another, explains the infinite variety of the sky, so different from that of France, still more from the English sky. I gazed from that window by day and by night upon a spectacle ever changing, ever splendid, save when one of those endless tempests of snow, of which those living in Europe can form no idea, was raging.   How can I describe the moon-light which suddenly followed those storms fleck-ing the half-frozen river in which pillars of fire were bathed?   I was only separated from it by the narrow garden covered with a white sheet. Every idea of earth vanished; I seemed to soar above that silver flood as freely as the gulls who appeared in flocks with the first rays of dawn.

These effects produced by the changing season and the varying atmosphere are inseparable in my memory from the delicious hospitality which lent them a festal character; and when people tell me that after all Boston is only a city of five hundred thousand inhabitants, merely the capital of Massachusetts,- I find it hard to believe them, in view of the royal phastasmagoria of the Charles River.   Those who love contrasts cannot do better than to visit Boston after Chicago, with-out a break.   They will abruptly breathe the atmosphere of the past.

If we walk through the old part of the town, crooked and irregular as it is, we might imagine ourselves in some old English city; the tangled iron wires of telegraph and telephone visible above the street, alone lend it an individual

aspect. Such districts as Commonwealth Avenue
or Beacon Street are broad avenues lined with
dwellings whose impressive architectural regularity is unimpaired by any showy ornamenta-
tion. These houses are entered from a porch
preceded by a flight of steps; over most of the
granite or sandstone fronts spreads the delicate
tapestry of a Japanese vine known as Boston ivy;
its reddish foliage, which in autumn becomes of
the color of coral, is a delight to the eye. Behind
the window-panes is a wealth of flowers, which
shows the elegance of those drawing-rooms where
people certainly talk better and in lower tones
than anywhere else in America. Having once
been the chief city in the Union, — and with
Philadelphia, the one which played the most
illustrious part in the Revolution, — Boston now
affects a somewhat provincial character; but this
provincialism, with which it is reproached by
those outside its fashionable and literary circles,
is in itself an attraction. Bostonians have made
their city, as it were, the casket for the noble
memories of a land whose history is as yet but
brief. They live with their eyes fixed on the
gilded dome of the State House, which contains so many honorable trophies; on the ancient
graveyard where citizens like Samuel Adams and

John Hancock sleep; on Bunker Hill Monument, which marks the spot where the British troops were held in check by 'prentice hands, who knew nothing of the art of war but that they must stand firm and shoot close. They pride them-selves on Faneuil Hall, that cradle of American liberty. The word "old" is constantly on their lips when they speak of their possessions. To be sure, their antiquity goes no farther back than the seventeenth and eighteenth centuries, and has left behind but few monuments worthy of the name; but, lacking these, Boston sets on foot ingenious plans for preserving and renewing patri-otic pride in the hearts of her children. This very year, on the night of April 19, a moving celebration took place in commemoration of Paul Revere's glorious ride, — the event which pre-ceded the Lexington fight, where Massachusetts militia-men and farmers got the better of English regulars. Signals were lighted this spring night at the north end of the town, in the little belfry of Christ Church, the same which in 1775 warned the country of the march of the British troops on Concord; and a rider, in the dress of the Colonial period, galloped over the six miles traversed by Paul Revere, calling to arms the sleeping farmers, who answered as of yore. The only difference was that now their cheers were mingled with fireworks; and when the long silent bells of the little North Church ·began to ring, every bell round about answered them in chorus. Such scenes are calculated to affect the most ignorant and insensible, and to develop in others a generous ardor.

We understand, if we live in Boston, and imbue our mind with its spirit, the sort of ill will which England still feels for the colony which escaped from her rule, — an ill will betrayed by a systematic blackening of everything American. Here, for instance, is a city where the English find the traces of their defeats preserved as precious relics, and where no less evident traces of their moral, intellectual, and literary influence endure, — a city both hostile and of close kin, whose every stone recalls one of those family quarrels which are the most violent of all. Plainly, it is far less easy to do it justice than to praise with contemptuous indulgence Chicago and her progress as of a new-born giant, to say nothing of the fact that Great Britain would be glad to claim a thinker like Emerson, a novelist like Hawthorne, both of whom are purely Bostonian, while at the same time they have added masterpieces to English literature. When we think of the long list of select spirits produced by Boston, it is impossible not to forgive her for becoming, from a very excess of her good qualities of enthusiasm and veneration, something like a great mutual admiration society. As for me, I can no more wonder at the anecdotes told of Longfellow, Lowell, Whittier, Bancroft, Prescott, Channing, and Theodore Parker, than at the pious care which marks by a bust or an inscription those spots in the city where Franklin, Daniel Webster, and Charles Sumner were born. The presence of the illustrious dead, to whom secret and constant worship is paid, adds to the somewhat solemn nature of Boston. The great dead seem to be even more alive than the living themselves; the living summon them up, quote them, talk of them on every occasion. Indeed, we are religiously shown the place occupied until 1876, among the ancient elms on the Common, by the oldest of them all, the Old Elm, before the foundation of the city; its shadow still rests upon it.

If Massachusetts, and especially Boston, be justly proud of the men to whom they have given birth, they are none the less honored as the parents of a group of women whose equals it

would be hard to find elsewhere. As far back as
the earliest Colonial days, we find names which
must ever be surrounded by an aureole of courage,
virtue, devotion to the new home. Anne Hutch-
inson was one of the first to break with established authorities, albeit it was only in the field
of religious argument. The wives of Adams,
Knox, and Hancock helped by their energy and
their personal sacrifices to establish independence; and it seems to me that one of the most
heroic dames is that Mrs. Cushing who at the time
of the declaration of rights was willing, with her
friends, to go dressed in the skins of wild beasts
rather than to buy English goods. Deborah
Sampson, who served in the ranks of the Revolutionary army, was also a native of Massachusetts. Never was the protest against slavery
more eloquent than in the mouths of Boston
women. Lydia Maria Child strove side by side
with those champions of liberty, Garrison and
Wendell Phillips; Maria W. Chapman lent the
lustre of her beauty and her spiritual power to
the good cause. During the war between North
and South, women everywhere outdid each other
in devotion; but the New England Woman's
Auxiliary Association furnished more than
$314,000 in money and supplies for Northern

soldiers.   Mrs. Livermore — whose name is well known as the president of the first congress for the advancement of women held by the Association — at that time organized the first of those Sanitary Fairs which produced such fruitful results.   Her double gift of pen and tongue, her tremendous activity were at the service of the Union throughout the war.   Clara Barton, head of the Red Cross movement; Susan B. Anthony and Lucy Stone, leaders of the Woman's Suffrage cause; the generous abolitionist, Lucretia Coffin Mott, — were all born in Massachusetts, although their influence spread far beyond her borders.

As for the Boston women who have worked to advance the science of education, how·can I name them all?   I shall try to show, when I describe my visits to various colleges, the impulse given to the Woman's Annex of Harvard University by Mrs. Agassiz, widow of the great naturalist. A daughter of Agassiz, Mrs. Shaw, also devotes her time to pedagogy with equal wisdom and generosity.   About the year 1860, Miss Elizabeth Peabody imported Frœbel's method.   Mrs. Shaw established and for fifteen years supported sixteen free kindergartens, which now belong to the city.   Under her direction, and thanks to her inexhaustible liberality, experiments of all

sorts have been tried, — manual work in public
schools, industrial schools, vacation schools, and
day nurseries. Her preparatory school for boys
and girls has long held a unique position. Here
we see a truly national spirit of independence and
enterprise. A desire to educate her own children
in her own way, outside the existing methods,
determined Mrs. Shaw to establish this school.

Mrs. Mary Hemenway deserves the utmost
praise for perceiving that feminine arts stood in
great need of encouragement in America, where
cooking and sewing are generally neglected for
love of Greek. She established practise lessons
in the public schools for the purpose of training
housewives; she devoted herself to re-establishing
a good condition of the wretched body, too often
despised by youthful scholars, adding gymnastics
to their other lessons. She fanned the flames of
patriotism by paying the cost of free lectures on
American history, to be given in the Old South
Church, filled with relics connected with that
history; she established the ground-work of the
first museum of American archæology.

In the field of Science, Massachusetts has pro-
duced an astronomer held in high esteem by
Herschel, Humboldt, and Le Verrier, — Maria
Mitchell; in art, a sculptor, — Arrne Whitney,

who has two of her statues in Boston public
squares; several painters (I visited the studios
of Miss Greene and Miss Bartol, Mrs. Sears and
Mrs. Whitman); and a famous actress, Charlotte
Cushman.   The first volume of American poetry
was by a woman, — Anne Bradstreet, in 1650.
Margaret Fuller — who wrote Latin verse at the
age of eight, who lectured in German, French,
and Italian, and bore a part in the best days
of transcendentalism, in the Fourieristic experiments at Brook Farm — opened that celebrated
conversation class whose influence still lives in
Boston.   Her object was to pass in review all
departments of knowledge, striving to mark the
relations existing between them, to systematize
thought, and to diffuse those qualities of precision
and clearness which are but too rare among
women.

MRS. JULIA WARD HOWE. — THE NEW
ENGLAND WOMAN'S CLUB.

Mrs. Julia Ward Howe ranks first, and that
not only by seniority.   I knew a number of
her works on social and other questions.   I knew
that for forty years her name had been a part of
every movement of the woman's cause in America,

— and yet I did not suspect the importance of the part which she played until a very simple incident revealed it to me.

An early morning sleigh-ride led me to a fine country mansion near Milton. After luncheon, I was chatting with Americans of the best society, most well-informed as to all European matters, although they do not pass the greater part of their life abroad as so many do, knowing too well how many necessary things yet remain to be done in their own country, in which it is their duty to assist. A most agreeable old man told anecdotes of his youthful experiences in Paris, and of the impression, still vivid, made on him by Rachel's singing, or rather declaiming, of the Marseillaise. All at once soft music was heard in a corner of the room, — a sort of military march, played by a young woman seated at the piano. I asked what it was, and found that it was the Battle Hymn of the Republic, the battle hymn of the Northern troops during the Civil War. At first, I was told, it was set to savage and sanguinary words, lines of vengeance inspired by the death of John Brown, — the old abolitionist farmer who undertook to rouse the blacks to revolt before the declaration of war, who took possession of a town with the aid of

twenty-two men, defended the arsenal so long as
a man of his little troop was left, and, covered
with wounds, was at last sentenced to be hanged,
his execution giving a tremendous impetus to the
question then pressing upon the people. "Old
John Brown" was in every mouth; Mrs. Howe,
changing the words, turned it into the Battle
Hymn. And when I asked to have it sung
two voices chanted it, soon accompanied by other
voices, — all present, young and old, joining in
the chorus with deep feeling; for there were
some present who took part in the war, others who
recalled losses dating back to the four years echo
which rang with this warlike hymn mingled with
trumpet blasts and the noise of cannon. Before the
last verse died away, — that verse which charges
men to die for freedom, as Christ died for them, —
I saw that America had a Marseillaise suited to her
temper and written by a woman, a rival of Mrs.
Beecher Stowe. Mrs. Stowe, hidden in a country
parsonage, dealt slavery a mortal blow when she
wrote the famous book whose fame spread around
the world. Mrs. Howe, in her turn, flung into
the heart of the conflict which ensued, a solemn,
sacred song which has ever since been to the
victorious North a national anthem.

My surprise was great when I afterwards met

the author of the Battle Hymn. I expected to see an old woman, — the date of her birth, 1819, being set down in all her biographies, — I know not why I had also attributed to her the somewhat masculine air of authority common to many strong minded women. I saw a smile, a skin, a look, which were all extraordinarily youthful. She dresses without the least eccentricity, she has simple and perfect manners, her gentle voice is one of the best modulated that I ever heard. If by chance Mrs. Howe had chosen to preach subversive doctrines, she would have been very dangerous, so potent are the tact and charm which make it possible for her to dare anything. I greeted her in her kingdom, the New England Woman's Club, over which she presides. The club was founded twenty-five years ago to afford a meeting place for the many ladies who live in the suburbs of Boston and who were called to Boston on business of any kind; this led to the institution of a weekly meeting at which various subjects are discussed: art, litera-ture, education, etc. These exercises assumed a growing importance as the number of the mem-bers grew; often speakers from outside joined in the discussions.

On the Monday in November when I entered

the spacious and comfortable quarters in Park
Street, I saw nothing to suggest the idea of
pedantry or pretence. I might have imagined
myself at a reception in a private house; there was
no platform, but an amply furnished tea-table.
Not nearly all of the two hundred and thirty members were present, but still there was a numerous
company, among whom was one man, the sole
survivor of the group of great masculine minds
who at the outset were allied with the club as
honorary members. The most distinguished
women of the city entered, one after another, and
Mrs. Howe presented them to the foreign visitors,— Miss Spence and myself. Miss Spence
is an Australian celebrity; she had just arrived
from her native land, very lively and very
spirited, with an air both rustic and intelligent, and lectured on the right of minor-
ities. We heard her talk on the way voting is
arranged in Australia. But Mrs. Howe chiefly
drew my attention. When the meeting opened,
the woman of the world showed herself as president. It would be impossible for me to describe
the quiet assurance or the polite authority of the
three little blows struck on the table with a
mallet to request silence. Her attitude might
be envied by more than one president of the

French Chamber of Deputies. She answered Miss Spence with the most brilliant of improvisations; then, business despatched, she returned to her cups of tea and her introductions with the exquisite grace of any mistress of a mansion.

In fact, there is no city where the feminine element is better represented than in Boston. I satisfied myself of that at all the agreeable luncheons which followed, now at Mrs. Howe's house, and now at the houses of other members of the Woman's Club. No gathering of women in France could have the same animation or would take such pains to be agreeable. The absence of men would make French women feel as a young Washington girl expressed it, — as if they were eating bread without butter. In Boston, on the contrary, a select set take pleasure in what they call — treating each other in sisterly fashion — their "magic circle." It is a great honor and a very great pleasure for a stranger to find temporary admission; but I must repeat, nothing could be more foreign to French habits. Imagine a dozen women forcing themselves, on a certain day, to talk another language than their own throughout luncheon, lest they should forget that language, or in order that they might perfect themselves in it! Some heresies, indeed, slip into their opinions of French matters.   One of them, for instance, told me that Frémiet's Joan of Arc was the finest statue in Paris; another considers Maeterlinck, all whose works she has read, to be an untutored genius. Did not the great Margaret Fuller rank Eugene Sue very close to Balzac?   A passionate admirer of George Sand, she thought the "Lettres d'un Voyageur" tolerably dull; she thought the "Sept Cordes de la Lyre" far superior; and one of her illustrious friends called Alfred De Vigny a boudoir author, judging him no doubt by the first pages of the "Histoire d'une Puce Enragée." Assuredly, we too often commit absurd blunders in our criticisms of foreign authors, but it is always comforting to learn that strangers make as many and as grave errors in regard to ours.

Mrs. Howe, indeed, does not differ from us in her point of view as much as do many of her fellow-countrywomen.   She shows the effects of a prolonged sojourn in France, of her relations with eminent Frenchmen; and she recalls all this in the French language, with which she is marvellously familiar.   Study and reflection have left her a wholly youthful spontaneity, seasoned with sprightliness.   It would be hard to find her match for wit.   I tried to lead her to talk of herself, but I was not very successful. It was from others that I learned the opposition which her early literary tastes encountered. Her father — a father of the old school — did not allow his daughters to make themselves singular; in fact it was not for some years after her marriage that she began the work of writing 'and speaking, which she still carries on. Julia Ward married Dr. Howe, the man who did most to promote the education of deaf mutes, and who developed such extraordinary powers in the famous Laura Bridgman, who was deaf, dumb, and blind. Laura Bridgman has now a rival, Helen Keller, taught by the same methods. Dr. Howe devoted himself with equal ardor to making the most of the feeblest ray of comprehension in idiots. I was told that for lack of time by day he formed an evening class for them, declaring that their poor brains had no knowledge of time: he never thought of his own fatigue. To the last day of his life, by dint of scientific and humanitarian zeal, he wrought true miracles. Mrs. Howe, meantime, followed in Margaret Fuller's footsteps, working in the cause of woman with the same ardor and discretion. We might say of her what was said of her predecessor and friend, that she never lent herself to any exaggeration; that she never considered woman as the rival or the antagonist of man, but as his complement, assuming that the advance of the one is inseparable from the advance of the other.

I heard Mrs. Howe speak one morning, as a strong but independent Christian, in a Unitarian Church. It is not unusual in America for women to preach; there are hundreds of women clergy. It is in the West particularly that they exercise their ministry; and it seems that the parishes of these ladies are by no means the least well governed. Even in Boston, where the official care of souls is wholly in the hands of men, women are admitted to a certain collaboration in some churches, or at least in their vestries. The vestry where Mrs. Howe, with her silvery and penetrating voice, spoke eloquently of things both divine and practical, was that of the Church of the Disciples. She spoke of personal religion, showing the utility of family worship, the good sides of certain observances whose necessity had long seemed to her doubtful, but to which she now does full justice. Never was absolute loyalty expressed in a more touching way. Mrs. Howe strove to prove that even those of us who thought ourselves stripped of the good things of this world have endless cause for gratitude to

God, were it only for His Son, for the free gift of certain affections, and first of all for that of intelligence.

After Mrs. Howe, the wife of the Rev. C. G. Ames, pastor of the church where we were gathered, spoke with singular ease and power. She took up in detail the subject of the gratitude which we owe not only to God but to our neighbor. Do we think enough of what we should be if those whom we call the lowly, the humble, and the ignorant did not help us to bear the burden of the physical tasks which fall to our daily lot? And the speaker numbered our obligations to servants and tradesmen, the living wheels in the machinery of existence, with whom we think, very unjustly, that we are quits when we have paid their wages. I already knew Mrs. Ames through the excellent statistics showing the state of every sort of female labor in Massachusetts. She is the chairman of a committee devoted exclusively to these questions.

Young mothers then rose, and asked and answered questions in regard to the religious education of their children, to their devotional habits at home, to books of familiar morals classed under the head of "little helps." There was an exchange of profitable experiences. It seemed to me that this must have been the fashion of the meetings of the first Christians, the more so that after the speeches and the hymns there were love-feasts, — love-feasts of American style. Tea was served in one of the aisles of the vestry, and Mrs. Ames laughingly asked me if I was not shocked to see that the church was connected with a kitchen.   I at once replied that I had seen more than that in the West, where the church, which is still the meeting-house, is often chosen as the scene of meetings which are of no religious nature.   I added that a lady in that part of the country, observing my surprise, said, like a good Puritan, "Nothing can be out of place in a church but dissipation; and dissipation is out of place everywhere."

The last time that I met Mrs. Howe was shortly before the success of the Municipal Woman Suffrage Bill which had passed to its third reading in the Massachusetts House of Representatives by a majority of 11.   She regarded this as prophetic of its adoption by the State legislature, and she was that day to demand, at some public meeting, the unrestricted right for the women of her country to vote, basing her demand on the excellent reason that they have long been prepared for it.

Mrs. Howe shows the same serene calm in

making claims of this kind that she does when she sets forth in church her theories of practical and individual Christianity.   Whatever theme she takes up, she is always temperate, showing no excitement, although a flame burns in her blue eyes which are still so youthful.   Since Lucy Stone's death, her importance as a leader seems to be still greater. We know that Lucy Stone was chairman of the executive committee of the "Association for the Suffrage of American Women," an association founded by her in 1869, with the aid of W. L. Garrison, G. W. Curtis, Colonel Higginson, Mrs. Livermore, and Mrs. Howe herself.

The curious history of this feminine pioneer is well worth writing.   As a mere child, she resolved to go to college to learn Greek and Hebrew, that she might study the Bible in the original, and find out whether the words which shocked her: "Thy desire shall be for thy husband, and he shall rule over thee," were really in the text.   She paid her way by manual labor, doing her own cooking, and paying but fifty cents a week for her room. On leaving Oberlin college, she devoted herself to teaching slaves escaped from their masters, and in 1847 she began her famous lectures on woman's rights, putting up her posters with her own hands, braving mockery and danger of every sort, stirring

crowds by her eloquence and the strange magnetism which seemed to proceed from her. Although
married to Henry Blackwell, himself a partisan
of woman's rights and the abolition of slavery,
she never bore her husband's name. Blackwell
approved her course; he joined his protest to hers
against the iniquity of the law which grants the
husband supreme authority over the person, property and children of his wife. Moreover, they
were for forty years the model of happy couples.

The bust of Lucy Stone, by Anne Whitney, at
the Chicago Exhibition, gives the idea of perfect
and sympathetic simplicity. When she died in
Boston, last October, her funeral, which took
place at the Unitarian Church of the Disciples,
seemed like a triumph. More than eleven hundred people assembled, and the services were
accompanied by striking manifestations. The Suffrage colors — yellow and white — were represented
by mounds of roses and chrysanthemums. Another
woman who played an active part in the crusade
against slavery, Mrs. Edna Dean Cheney, whom
I had the honor to meet at Mrs. Howe's house,
spoke of Lucy Stone better than any one else,
contrasting her with two or three persons whose
names always come up in Europe whenever American Suffragists are mentioned. Mrs. Cheney, too,

has been an ardent apostle of the emancipation of women; but her energy now seems to be centred in the admirable New England Hospital for women and children, where all the doctors are women. Mrs. Cheney is at the head of the board of council, and is one of the directors.

We know that the first Medical School for women was opened in Boston in 1848. At that time there was no other in the world; now it is incorporated with the medical faculty of the Boston University. The city of Boston now has thirty-nine allopathic and forty-one homœopathic women doctors, besides eighty-nine practising without a diploma; for Massachusetts has no law in regard to the practice of medicine. We shall meet with these irregular practitioners elsewhere.

MISS ANNA TICKNOR. — SOCIETY FOR THE EN-
COURAGEMENT OF STUDY AT HOME. — PUBLIC
LIBRARIES.

Miss Ticknor represents a very original work, which she was the first to undertake, and which has quietly achieved almost incalculable results. I mean the society for the Encouragement of Study at Home. She took the first idea of this society from England, where clever minds had hit upon a great truth; namely, that work is the most essential element of happiness, and that those who do not have to work for a living, and are incapable of finding some absorbing occupation, are quite as much to be pitied as if they were poor. At first, she only intended to guide by correspondence young girls who had just left school, and so to help them to continue their intellectual life, which is too often quickly abandoned. Then her idea broadened. "It seemed to me," she says, "that we might succeed in adding to the fundamental value of home for all women, even the humblest, by giving them an opportunity to think; by familiarizing them with the conceptions of great minds which should keep them company while their hands are busy with their daily tasks. It seemed to me that it would be well for such women to open their eyes to the wonders of Nature in the most remote and desert country regions, and to appreciate art, if by chance they should encounter it."

In 1873, six ladies pledged themselves to correspond with forty-five persons who were then entered as students. Now one hundred and ninety lady teachers are in friendly relations with four hundred and twenty-three students; to say nothing of forty-six clubs, represented by a single name,

behind which is a numerous group who have combined for reasons of economy, to which is added
the pleasure of working in company. Each pupil
is treated according to her special requirements,
although a uniform rule is followed, — her cor-
respondent belonging to one section or another of
one of the six departments which make up the
round of studies, each of which has a head. The
work consists of reading and making notes ; the
result is shown by a monthly correspondence including frequent examinations. A small annual
fee, to pay office expenses and postage, provides
for the circulation of some two thousand volumes.
Usually but one subject, two at the utmost, are
taken up, the intelligent directors of the work
having a peculiar dread of that superficial and
indiscriminate culture which is a common defect
in America. Each student chooses one of six
departments. History is divided into five sections ;
the section of ancient history includes classic literature, and even Greek and Latin authors, the necessary aid being given, if desired, for the study of
those languages. Political economy does not
exclude the theory and history of philanthropy.
Science includes all its branches, embracing
hygiene, which explains why so many American
women are so learned in regard to questions of

drainage, heating, lighting, and ventilation.   In the
natural sciences, the methods of Professor Agassiz
are used : the pupils study specimens, not books.
Herbals, collections of all sorts, are sent from one
to another; as are portfolios of photographs and
engravings, for those students who choose the
third course, — that of the fine arts.   In connection
with the course in art, there is a section for imaginary travels in Europe, which in that land of pre-
eminent activity is a delight to all women too poor
or too ill to travel in reality.   The fourth department is devoted to German; the fifth to the study
in French, of French history and literature ; the
sixth to English literature, the section of rhetoric
having a long list of pupils, whose compositions
are carefully read and corrected.

May I be permitted, while admiring the rest, to
express the wish that the French library may be
enlarged ?   Our great writers are scarcely represented save by fragments and through the criticisms
of English authors.   Sainte-Beuve is the only one
who is complete; still, I found to my great pleasure a few volumes of Bossuet, Racine, and La
Bruyère.   In America our seventeenth century
is despised.   It would be a patriotic work, it seems
to me, to send a good collection of unexpurgated
French classics to the Library of the Studies at

Home. An intellectual fellowship which would redound to our glory would thus add to the good already accomplished by this Society, which achieves such manifold results.

The developement of taste extends to every detail of life. Mothers are prepared to play the part of teachers; and for the many daughters who do not marry, what a precious resource it must be! I remember the happy face of a certain elderly spinster whom I met in a cold village of that New England whose long winters must bring unspeakable boredom to those who have no absorbing occupations. She lived for that correspondence which connected her with the world, with the best that the world can offer. Without leaving her fireside, she travelled; she kept herself well informed; she satisfied that intellectual hunger which is as urgent with some as physical hunger. And I could not help wishing that some of the idle, discontented women in French provincial towns could have the same resource. All social conditions are represented among the students; one of them wrote from afar these touching words: "At night, when I have copied my lesson and hung it on my kitchen wall, I find it no longer tires me to wash up the dishes."

Many of these correspondences go on for ten,

twelve, and even eighteen years. Friendship often follows between the women thus brought together. Some scholars rise to the rank of teachers; they are mutually helpful. Thus a poor deaf mute, destitute of almost everything, proved herself a skilful botanist, and found a lucrative position suited to her bent. Other societies have been formed in various parts of America in imitation of this one, of which Miss Anna Ticknor is the active manager. The most extraordinary manifestation of the kind is the popular movement at Chautauqua; but that is one of the vast and rough-hewn schemes of the West, and the eminently Bostonian drawing-room in Marlboro' Street is no place to discuss it. The chief ornament of the parlor is a portrait of Sir Walter Scott by Leslie, who painted it expressly for Miss Ticknor's father, the well-known author of an excellent History of Spanish Literature. Having visited Europe, he greatly pleased Walter Scott, who at his request sat for this admirable work, of which England possesses merely a miniature copy.

I had instructive talks with Miss Ticknor. It is not in vain that one is the heiress of a race of scholars, the daughter of that Professor Ticknor who, the owner of a fine collection of books, by lending them freely, practised the rarest sort of charity for a book-lover. She was thus able to procure for me many details in regard to an interesting subject, that of free public libraries. There are three hundred and fifty-two cities in the State of Massachusetts, and three hundred have a free library, — that is, one permitting books to be taken out by citizens of the town; and there are almost two hundred women librarians, and many more women assistants. Almost all these libraries were established by private efforts, although now the government grants a certain sum of money to small towns in arrears. Special gifts of money, not to mention books, exceed five million dollars. And these free libraries not only help to diffuse learning, they annually collect all documents relating to the city, — genealogies, family annals, publications of every description appertaining to the social, moral, political, or economic growth of the population.

Of course the great Boston Public Library is the crown and capstone of the system, and a model for the whole United States. Strange to say, it has grown up about some books sent from Paris in 1840, and given by a Frenchman named Vattemare. A decided impulse to its growth was imparted by George Ticknor. It is now the most important free public library in the world; it has almost two million volumes in circulation, and is soon to be transferred to the worthy monument now almost finished in Boston's principal square, — Copley Square, — close beside the Museum of Fine Arts, and opposite Trinity Church, that masterpiece by Richardson, adorned with superb windows by La Farge, Burne Jones, and William Morris.

MRS. J. T. FIELDS. — DRAWING-ROOMS AND INTERIORS.

After what I have said of the resources of Boston society, to which the University town of Cambridge lends efficient aid, my readers must have reasoned correctly that in that city of old European traditions there must be interesting drawing-rooms. I would fain describe the one which, from many points of view, most resembles the drawing-rooms of France at its best, — the drawing-room of Mrs. J. T. Fields. To speak of Mrs. Howe, Mrs. Agassiz, Miss Ticknor, and Mrs. Fields is to speak of the social movement, — of culture, pedagogy, poetry, and philanthropy in Boston. They are the representatives of these things, and as such they must accept the publicity which clings to their personality. I therefore hope that I may not be reproached with indiscretion if I introduce the French public to a registry office for wits of the most refined originality, — a house unique in its way. Everything in it seems to be dedicated to literature. This is not surprising, Mrs. Annie Fields being the widow of the well-known publisher, James T. Fields, who was the friend of the most famous writers of his time in France and England, and who left behind him precious proofs of his intimacy with them all, — biographical notes, sketches, letters, conversations.[1] Their portraits cover the walls of this little temple of memory, where a woman of the utmost distinction carefully preserves all which represents to her a past of pure intellectual happiness. The riches of the library, which invade two floors of her small but delightful home, may be numbered, with an almost endless collection of autographs, among the treasures of which she is justly proud. As for her own works, she often shows excessive modesty in concealing them. These occasional works, which are like a rare embroidery on the woof of the charitable tasks to which she is particularly devoted, lead Mrs. Fields by preference towards Greek antiquity. Indeed, we might note some curious analogies between the bent of her talent and the character of her beauty, which years have merely spiritualized without destroying.

[1] Biographical Notes and Personal Sketches. Yesterdays with authors.

This Athenian of Boston lives in the company
of Sophocles and Eschylus, translates the Pandora
of Gœthe, that other Greek of Northern climes;
and the " Centaur " by Maurice de Guérin, who
also partook in France of Attic honey; and
she will figure on her own account in future
anthologies, were it only for her poem of " Theo-
critus,"[1] to say nothing of the recollections of her
dead friends which she writes. Thus, last year,
she published an animated and charming biography
of Whittier, the Quaker poet. Prose and verse
seem to be carelessly flung off by Annie Fields,
when the inspiration seizes her, upon loose leaves
covering the desk in the tiny study, which is
wholly unpretending, and is only divided by a
curtain from the parlor where so many illustrious
writers have been seated, and where such brilliant
converse has been held with friends like Hawthorne, Emerson, Longfellow, and Holmes.

The latter, old in years, but not in spirit, till
very recently survived the elect group to which
he belonged. His visits were always considered
a genuine treat. He brought with him the lively
sallies, the amusing digressions, which abound in
those essays so ingeniously brought together in the
Autocrat, the Professor, and the Poet at the Break-

[1] Under The Olive.

fast Table. Paris was ever present to him through
the charm of his youthful years; he talked of it
with as much gayety as if he were still a medical
student in the Latin Quarter. It was a pleasure
to find in the vivid and brilliant little person of
that amazing old man a combination of the perfect
gentleman of Old England with those qualities of
animation, sympathy, wholly cosmopolitan comprehension of things, and a wealth of amiability
which, we must admit, belong far more to New
England. The existence of Dr. Holmes must
have been both enviable and fatiguing. He was
at the same time venerated like a grandfather, and
treated like a spoiled child. Hospitable dames
contended for his presence. Passing strangers
requested permission to call on him, owners of
autograph albums, whose name is legion, begged
for a sentiment or a sonnet in his beautiful, dis-
tinct handwriting. At every public ceremony a
speech was expected from him; at every banquet he was requested to offer a toast; and ladies
combined to send him exquisite symbolic gifts, to
which he could only reply by invoking at any cost
the Muse of his best days to answer in a fashion
no less exquisite. This was putting the powers
of an octogenarian to a rude test; but he did not
seem to suffer from it, and gallantly quaffed the

nectar of adulation poured into the loving cup, in the bottom of which are engraved the names of his fair and learned friends.

Miss Sarah Jewett, whose life is divided between the Maine village which she has made immortal, in tales which emanate from the very soil itself, and Boston which claims her as its own, is almost always present at Mrs. Fields's Saturday afternoon receptions.

There too I met T. B. Aldrich, best known in France as a novelist, through the translations which have appeared in the " Revue des Deux Mondes," but whose poetic work — which has won him a place apart in the loftiest regions of the American Parnassus — is as inaccessible to translation as Gautier's " Émaux et Camées " could possibly be. And he excels not only in carving on hard stone, with singular technical skill, some tiny poem, perfect in all its parts, like his " Intaglio of a Head of Minerva," which the most experienced artists of the Old World might envy him. No one has so strong a feeling for Nature as he, that American Nature which is so unlike any other. Dr. Holmes was quite right to say, " You may search elsewhere in vain for a Boston sunset." American skies have nothing in common with those of Europe; birds, rocks,

earth, trees, grass, all are different. Well, though
he has travelled so far, it is yet to the New England spring, to the rivers decked with Indian
names, to the snows, the rains, the twilights of
Boston that Thomas Bailey Aldrich owes his truest
and best inspirations.   Perhaps his flights are somewhat short: we should not complain of this ; the
brevity of his pieces is a warrant of perfection.
Neither should we regret that the elegance and
ease of his existence have limited the possibility
of his effort; if fruitful poverty had borne him
company, he might never have written that enchanting and humorously melancholy piece, " The
Flight of The Goddess."

Cambridge sends to Mrs. Fields's parlors, with
young and brilliant professors, one of the notabilities of the academic town, whose name has crossed
the seas, — he who was first the Reverend, then
Colonel, Wentworth Higginson.   Madame de Gas-
parin once translated his " Military Life in a Black
Regiment," and his " History of the United States
for Young People " is popular in France.   Possibly
the nations of conventional old Europe are less
able to understand some of the ideas which he
expresses under the title " Common Sense about
Women ; " and Colonel Higginson would be the
last to wonder at this, fully aware as he is of the

lamentable situation of woman in countries where
the Salic law flourishes, where the masculine sex
is still called the " noble sex." His advice in regard to progress in the condition of woman is this :
" Let us first remove all artificial restrictions; it
will then be easy, for men as well as women, to
acquiesce in the natural limits imposed."

In the drawing-room to which I have introduced
you, — a green drawing-room, long and narrow,
with windows at either end, and a matchless view
over the Charles River, — a wood fire, such as we
have in France, burns on the hearth, but does not
prevent the gentle warmth of a furnace, which permits of the absence of doors, for which drawn
curtains are substituted, so that visitors pass in
quietly and unceremoniously from the staircase,
which is in full sight, taking their place at once
in the conversation.   Busts and portraits of famous
friends seem to form a part of the circle, — Wordsworth, the Brownings; Miss Mitford, with her fresh
bright face, the face of an elderly English spinster; Charles Dickens, painted by Alexander in
his youth with long hair and a coat of feminine
cut, which make him look like George Sand.   Mr.
Fields and his wife visited Europe more than once.
Thackeray as well as Dickens was their guest in
Boston: here is his friendly face, with its flat fea-

tures and his broad-shoulders.   Often an autograph letter is framed with the picture; this is the case with Mrs. Cameron's marvellous photograph of Carlyle, with its intense, pathetic expression.   Emerson thoroughly realizes in his appearance the idea of immateriality which I had formed of him.   Mrs. Fields tells me a pretty story of him.   In his later life, he was seized with a violent fit of curiosity; he wanted to know for once what rum was, and he went to the tavern to ask for it.   "Would you like a glass of water, Mr. Emerson?" said the barkeeper, without giving him time to express his guilty desire; and the philosopher drank his glass of water — and died without knowing the taste of rum.

Hawthorne, on the contrary, is superbly handsome, a substantial beauty, moustachioed and long-haired, which somewhat disconcerts us on the part of that sharp analyst of spiritually morbid and almost intangible things.   Longfellow has the head of a mild Jupiter; Lowell has the face of an English aristocrat.   Portraits of Dickens at various ages, and as utterly unlike as possible, hang in all directions.   Mrs. Fields gives us most curious accounts of his readings in America, where he was immensely successful.   The description of a huge gold chain which he fastened to his watch to hypnotize the attention of his hearers, went further than anything else to show me a certain vein of quackery which was combined with the novelist's undeniable talent; but I kept my opinion to myself, for it would not be well to meddle with the idols in the sanctuary which is sacred to them.

Having spoken of Mrs. Fields's drawing-room, it is hard to mention any other, although there are many houses in Boston where good talkers may be found, and hospitality (that common virtue in America) is nowhere more gracefully practised. I will merely allude to the effect of intellectual culture, carried to its utmost, upon the insides of houses, their furnishing and decoration. A sober elegance is the distinctive feature of that society which desires to show refinement in everything. The splendors of luxury are certainly not foreign to it; but their lustre is tempered, subdued as it were by good taste, as is not always the case elsewhere. For instance, I might mention one specially wealthy home which might easily have resembled some gorgeous curiosity shop or some showy museum of decorative art. It was the height of tact to avoid this rock, so to arrange that there is not too much of anything. From the altar screens taken from Italian churches to the French eighteenth-century trinkets and toys, from the

masterpieces of French and German painting to
the portrait of the mistress of the house (the finest
ever painted by Sargent), everything is in its
place, — everything, even a flag which belonged
to the grenadiers of Napoleon's guard, which
seems to recount the glories of the French army
to the corner of a renaissance mantelpiece. There
is no crowding, no confusion, no show ; a masterly
harmony pervades the whole; it is simply the
exquisite setting for a charming woman. Other
houses, — for instance, the one containing a fine
collection of paintings by the great colorist
William Hunt, — would appear to advantage in
the Faubourg St. Germain and are the homes of
stately dowagers, who would be by no means
out of place there.

This irreproachable taste seems to extend to
diet in a way which justifies the theories of Bril-
lat-Savarin. In America there is plenty of poor
cooking even in very rich houses, where the principal desire seems to have been to match the color
of the ices and the sauces to the color of the china
and the be-ribboned flowers which cover the table;
but in Boston the pursuit of outward elegance in
no way impairs the excellence of the substantial
part. There are, of course, certain things which
astonish a foreigner, — the early breakfast of solid

meats ; the grape-fruit, that huge, juicy Florida orange, served as a first course; the abuse of ice-water; heresies in the matter of wines. Still, we may say that the bill of fare on Boston tables shows that the mistresses of the houses have travelled much, and have brought back the best receipts from every country in Europe, grafting them upon native dishes which have their merits, like baked beans, — to mention only that very simple dish, which is as difficult of imitation as is the no less simple Creole way of cooking rice.

THE ISLAND.—ALMSHOUSES.—TENEMENT-HOUSES. —BOYS' BRIGADES.—ASSOCIATED CHARITIES.

The charitable organizations of Boston are almost numberless; and during the first weeks of my stay in that city I attributed the seeming suppression of pauperism to their wonderful activity. "And yet," I said to one of the women who devote their lives most eagerly to benevolent works, "you only help those who deserve it by helping themselves. What becomes of the others, — those who refuse to work, the waifs and strays of all degrees in the social scale, who evade the observance of any rule? There are beggars in every great city. What do you do with that class of people?" she replied: "They are sent to the

Island." And she quoted the words of an eminent professor who has established ethical precepts for social progress: " A certain part of the population can never be called free, in the sense that the education of poor children should be, in spite of the parents if need be, directed by society in a progressive fashion, and that that same society has the right to enslave all those who wilfully choose a vagabond life. The time has passed when kindly souls gave the tramp food and shelter. Every tramp in a civilized country should be arrested and compelled to work under public guidance."

Thus then is purchased, to the detriment of personal independence and caprice, what the best and most intelligent citizens of a republic call universal liberty. It is instructive to consider this. May we, however, in spite of social progress, never attain to this degree of severity; may we always permit beggars to find refuge on our church steps, in memory of the beautiful Christian legends of poverty. A church which does not freely admit the ragged poor to pray side by side with the rich, could never in our eyes be wholly the house of the Lord. In America, Protestants and Catholics alike told me that the decent and respectable poor could readily obtain proper clothes to wear to church ; but are those who are not " respectable " forbidden to pray, or even to warm their shivering limbs while they listen to organ tones and almost unconsciously absorb some crumbs of goodness? The old Middle Ages knew a sort of liberty foreign to purely modern lands, and we hope that we may always retain vestiges thereof amid our democratic acquisitions.

Correctional institutions are not the only ones to be found on the islands in Boston harbor; the poor-houses are also relegated to Long Island. I shall never forget the impression produced upon me one morning last spring by the bright sunny aspect of the harbor. Beyond the many ships at anchor, the islands lay scattered picturesquely, all close together; they seemed to have no other purpose than to add to the beauty of the panorama, while the winding, indented coast-line, stretched in promontories and peninsulas far down Massachusetts Bay and faded away in the blue distance. But I knew that each of those dots was the repository of those moral off-scourings of which the city is so carefully cleared; that mendicity and vice are driven there. I knew too that a scandal had lately broken out in Boston revealing dreadful abuses in the administration of those sad refuges. And if justice were done, it was, here again, due to a cry of warning and alarm uttered by a woman.

To Mrs. Lincoln belongs the honor of denouncing what went on in the hospital for the poor of Long Island, and investigation revealed plenty of odious details.

Mr. and Mrs. Lincoln, wealthy people always active in great Boston charities, dare on occasion to lift the thick veil cast in America over ugly and unmentionable things. The work to which these two philanthropists are especially devoted is that of tenement-houses, — an important problem. The tenement-house, swarming with tenants, is to the Anglo-Saxon a genuine hell. He requires — and foreigners can hardly understand the want, being of a more sociable temperament — a dwelling apart, small as it may be, where he need not dread contact with his neighbors; he needs what we cannot translate into French, — the privacy of the home, private life surrounded by walls within which he is master. Mr. and Mrs. Lincoln thought that for want of something better, the tenement-house itself might be improved, made compatible with family life. They have therefore bravely pledged themselves to the management of a number of houses, which they put in good condition, and where they exercise a watchful care greatly to the advantage of honest tenants who are thus rid of bad neighbors.

I was invited to an interesting meeting at their house. A Mr. Riis, a writer and lecturer of Dutch origin, read a short tale of his own, entitled "Skippy," — the pathetic story of a street boy who ended on the gallows, although he was born with all the qualities which go to make up a good American. The secret of his shipwreck lay in the fact that he had no home, no playground where children eager for play have full leave to throw a ball. Skippy sees beneath the black cap, at the final moment, not the crimes for which he is scarcely responsible; no, he sees the wretched tenement-house, the first cause of all his ills. The comments accompanying this story are all the more weighty because Mr. Riis, if I am not mistaken, has long filled an important place among the police. When he had ended, various persons spoke of miserable and forsaken children, — among others a young woman from Buffalo, who has given her life to moral work in the suburbs of that manufacturing town, which is most corrupt, according to the details which she unhesitatingly gives us in regard to the prostitution of six-year-old children. This is even worse than Chicago, where the Woman's Club had some difficulty in having the legal age of consent for girls changed from ten to sixteen.

One of the ladies present said to me: " I will take you to see my Skippys. You shall see what we make of them." And truly she did take me on the following Saturday, between seven and eight in the evening, to the big dance-hall, or something of the sort, which she has hired in the heart of a crowded district for the work of her brigade. This brigade is made up of street urchins, of whom she hopes to make men by following the receipt of Professor Drummond, who has covered England, and subsequently America, with well-disciplined companies. Little scamps who have never been to Sunday-school, who have not the faintest idea of obedience or respect, are invited in. They are attracted by the bait of a mock uniform, which they are not allowed to wear until they have learned the drill. All boys, from one end of the world to the other, have a natural taste for playing soldier. By degrees, while they learn to drill according to the manual, they also learn that a soldier should never have dirty hands, unkempt hair, or torn clothes; they learn punctuality and submission to rule. But what patience is needed on the part of the officers! Two Harvard students, familiar with military drill, undertook to form the stubborn brigade whose acquaintance I made that night. We saw before us a herd of small vagabonds, most

of whom wore shoes trodden down at the heels
and far too big for them, with the help of which
they dealt each other fearful kicks. They were
all beginners, and made the drill an excuse for
endless tricks; it would be impossible to silence
them. A row at last broke out, obliging the
officers to clear the hall in order to divide the ring-
leaders from those who showed a desire to learn.
In vain the generous manager of the brigade
tries to address them; in vain she shows them
the interesting pictures illustrating an article on
Professor Drummond's method, in McClure's magazine. They shout "toy soldiers!" when they
see the models held up to them; and they laugh
aloud, and hurl every weapon which comes to hand,
including the spittoons, at each other's heads! It
is always so in the beginning. Gavroche in America is terrible indeed, and he does not disguise
it. Craft seems as foreign to him as deference.
He impudently mocks at the wise men and fair
women who tire themselves in trying to help
him; but at least he never dreams of deceiv-
ing them by hypocritical and interested shams.
There must be several weeks of conflict with the
deviltries of these untaught savages; their fear
of being expelled conquers them; they become
worthy to wear the glorious insignia. After that,

it is as easy to lead them as a single man. We
see brigades going to the bath keeping step. We
see them start for one of those country encamp-
ments which are a part of American customs, the
poorest dweller in cities being thus enabled to
obtain a few days of rest and fresh air, to have a
profitable vacation which costs little or nothing.
I have read that the growth of these brigades was
nowhere so remarkable as in San Francisco, and
that four hundred boys, without supervision, formed
a summer camp on the shore of the Pacific Ocean,
one hundred and twenty-eight miles away from
the city. These boys had reached the degree of
Christian manliness which is held up to them as
an objective point, and which implies, above all,
self-respect; they were recognized as capable of
self-guidance. The paternal influence of a good
officer may do much to bring about this end, but
feminine influence also plays its part.

It is a pleasure to every active and resolute
young American woman to help in the formation
of this army of duty. I remember my surprise
the first time that the mother of a family said to
me in the most natural way: " One of my daughters has a taste for kindergartening; she gives all
her mornings to the care of children. Another
manages a boys' brigade." I had another oppor-

tunity to see how common this kind of charity is. The kind-hearted daughter of a rich publisher took me to the club, where the members enlisted under her command, have books, games, a gymnasium, and a small theatre. Escorting me afterwards through one of the finest printing-houses in the world, — the Riverside Press at Cambridge, — she introduced me with pride to one of her boys for whom she had found work with her father, a zealous assistant in the good mission which wholly absorbs her. Perhaps it is really to women that it belongs to shape men; the maternal instinct with which almost all of them are born prepares them for that task.

I admire more and more the public spirit shown on every occasion by Boston women ; no affair of city or state is foreign to them ; they labor untiringly at the wheel of progress. One of them, explaining to me how little she, for her own part, cared to have her sex allowed to vote, alleged this reason : " I should no longer feel free to apply to all our politicians for whatever I want." And what she wants, what they all want, is the general welfare; never giving way, even in matters of charity, to the blind impulse of a kind heart; having ever before them the great social problems, especially two great dangers which

should be contended against in every country, —
the collection of incapable people in great cities,
and the confusion too often occurring between the
unfortunates who should be helped and those made
miserable through their own fault, who should be
reformed. Europeans would be amazed to see
how easily this reform undertaken by American
philanthropy is applied to the character of people
for the better comprehension of their situation.
Drunkenness is the social evil; well, a drunkard
may be confined in the Inebriate Hospital and
receive medical treatment until he has made up
his mind to work for his family. I met at the five-
o'clock tea-table, at an elegant reception, a delicate
young woman who gives most of her time to the
hospital for drunkards. I had several talks with
a lady belonging to the best circles of Boston
society, whose especial mission is to visit the men's
prison. She enters their cells by special permission, talks with the prisoners, and acquires extraordinary influence over them. She courageously
spent some time locked up with a murderer whom
no one could manage, and who was as unable as
the rest to resist her words and her vigorous compassion. It is enough to look at her to understand
the power which she wields. Still beautiful with
her white hair, her eagle eyes full of fire, a sort of

kindly bluntness, an expression of force, of passion,
of enthusiasm throughout her whole being, she
is the personification of fearlessness. She dreads
nothing, and has no cause to dread anything.
Her tone is not always that of gentle and commonplace exhortation; she talks to these outcasts of the temptations and fatalities which are not
spared those whom they consider as the privileged
of the world; she shows them that all men are
alike after all, that all should strive, that victory
is alike difficult for all. I have heard her, and I
think I can vouch for the efficacy of the means
which she uses to move the hardened souls who
listen to her words. One of them, having left
prison after ten years' stay there, and reformed far
from his home, came to her in his new guise of an
honest man, to tell her that she alone had saved
him from suicide and despair, and that whatever
he had become he owed to her. "That," she
said, when she told me this incident, " is one of
those rewards which atone for everything."

I was present at a meeting of the " Boston Associated Charities," whose object is to insure the
harmonious action of the various benevolent societies to prevent begging, to study in wholly
scientific fashion the best methods of preventing
want. "Not alms, but a friend," — such is the

motto of this Association. It finds work, removes poor debtors from the clutches of usurious money-lenders, — the usurer being, with whiskey, the worst enemy of the American people.

This year (1894) being a year of exceptional suffering for the poor, in consequence of financial panics, the stoppage of production and the closing of many manufactories, the Association was also forced to work with exceptional zeal. In the discussion of the cases of poverty which took place during my visit, the part played by one of the ladies present particularly impressed me. The kind of charity which she exercises proves how much the study of languages does to enlarge the heart and mind, multiplying, as it were, the souls. If she did not understand all the tongues of Europe, Miss Alger might have been a Boston Puritan, weighing good and evil in the scales with strict justice; but she has become the interpreter in ordinary of wretched foreigners. She has made herself the advocate of their wants, of their feelings, which they cannot change from one day to another under the influence of the new atmosphere which they breathe. The Italians in particular are her children; she gives them back what she can of their absent home; she listens to them; she submits herself to be blamed for them, by excusing the worst points in those poor wrecks who in Boston streets remind us all too vividly of Naples or Palermo. I said that every one was concerned about the worthy poor. Miss Alger is possibly the only one interested in the unworthy poor; she loves them for their very weaknesses and their sins. Belonging myself to the corrupt Old World whence these emigrants come, I am as grateful to her as if I were one of them.

COLLEGE SETTLEMENTS. — REST CURE. — CHRISTIAN SCIENCE. — BOSTON FADS.

Of course this public spirit which is so common in America is particularly apparent in elderly people more or less free from the cares of housekeeping, unmarried or widowed persons, and mothers who are at liberty during school hours (American children being universally sent out of the house to school); still, it is not wholly lacking in young girls. I wish that French girls could see all that occupies the life of their American sisters besides the famous flirtation, and very often to its exclusion. In the first place, as a matter of course, they almost all belong to several clubs, — they would amount to nothing otherwise, — and the duties of a club are always absorbing. They are at once of an intellectual and a charitable order. Did not the members of the Young Ladies Saturday Morning Club once perform a tragedy by Sophocles? They found their model at Harvard, where the students, towards the close of my stay in Boston, played Terence in Latin, with all the details of learned archaism. The young women modestly confined themselves (and I am surprised at that) to a translation from the Greek. Undeniably the loveliest of the actresses, she whose statuesque attitude, with uplifted arms and eyes Mrs. Whitman's brush has caught,—a young Diana, who might have contented herself to play the part of a divinity, — by her own desire, solely from a wish to make herself useful, spends the better part of her days as an unpaid teacher in a school, and that quietly, never even alluding to it. Another, who might also feel proud of her beauty since the famous sculptor, St. Gaudens, begged her to pose for the figure of an angel, is utterly devoted to hospitals for children, and has written treatises on the proper care of babies. Still others, and many of them, are interested in college settlements. They appreciate the words of an English philanthropist: " How strange, almost unreal, our faint impalpable sorrows, our keen, painful, pet emotions seem in comparison with the great mass of abject misery which defiles our great cities ! "

Through the mouth of Mr. Robert Woods, an eloquent protest was sent from Andover House, that centre of Boston charity, against selfish, heartless learning. We would fain breathe it in the ears of all the vainglorious who imagine that intellectual labor exempts them from loving their fellow-men and from sacrificing themselves for them. The gist of it was as follows: Modern society has great resources thus far ill applied to manifold wants; we must balance resources and wants, and set in motion the forces of civilization: this is the best of all politics. But society cannot be saved by *methods;* it may be by *individuals.* It requires individual influence, continued intimacy, the interest taken in human affairs by those who have drunk at the fountain-head of knowledge, who have acquired the requisite philosophic and historic breadth to love their neighbor well. The knowledge acquired, far from deterring from the exercise of philanthropy, will merely add a further stimulus to natural pity. Each of us, without exception, should be an apostle.

I wish I could quote all the excellent things which Mr. Woods has written about the idea of the University Settlement; we should find many points in common with the social settlement as conceived by Miss Addams at Hull House. The object always is to make the labor of the poor attractive, the life of the poor agreeable. It is important that man should everywhere begin to visit other men, his brothers; that each visitor should be an angel of strength, showing his weaker brother the ignominy of a vicious life, and affording him, by his own example, a vision of a better life. Mr. Woods would like to see two establishments of this sort in every crowded district, — one for men and one for women. In Boston there are several. The first which I visited was small as to the size of the house, but as great as any other if we consider the ardor brought by the residents to their work; for, of course, mere visitors are not enough. The house must be occupied by persons giving all their time to it, ready to communicate with their neighbors of various conditions at any moment, day or night. Certain residents, who have resources of their own, are unpaid; others are supported by members of universities and by charitable citizens.

I reached the settlement, which to me will always be that of " the little blind girl," just between daylight and dark. The little blind girl, a child of six or seven, was seated in the lap of a young woman who was telling her a story while she rocked to and fro in her chair. At our approach she sprang up, with the freedom of a merry child, ran to us, stretching forth her poor hands like the antennæ of an insect to ward off possible obstacles. In an instant she had counted us, had made up her mind in regard to each, begging us to take off our gloves that she might feel our hands, and chattering of all sorts of things as if she had seen them. " She is the delight of the house," said one of the residents. " Her parents gave her to us, as they have a number of boys who made a perfect little martyr of their sister." Other children come and go from the street where snow is falling, into the little warm sitting-room. Some bring a penny for the bank, where their savings are growing by degrees. This may be the beginning of a virtue which was long unknown in America, that land of careless waste. Visitors also come one after another, — young women of the middle class, who, though pale and tired, still desire to help others after a hard day's work: one gives lessons; another is employed in an office, but living in the neighborhood, she stops to hear the news of this big family on her way home; a university graduate may also prove that four years of the higher studies have not set her apart from the common lot.

The second settlement to which I was introduced contained several pretty rooms, each of which was

furnished by one of the colleges for women in
Massachusetts. The lady in charge of the establishment tells us that she allows her assistants the
utmost possible freedom ; that no strict rule is
needed, but merely to oppose the organized forces
of good to the organized forces of evil, without
fear of soiling one's hands by attacking the moral
miseries which are but too often the almost inevitable results of extreme poverty. She and her comrades devoted themselves to a thorough study
of the social conditions of their district; then, once
familiar with the habits and the tasks of their neighbors, all was easy: they had only to enter into
communication with the charitable works already
existing in the vicinity, — with the trades-unions,
the workingmen's clubs, the temperance societies,
— to visit the sick, to talk, to lend books, to suggest healthy amusements.

In the next room we hear a confused chatter.
That room is full of little children; they spend
their afternoon in apparently childish fashion, but
after all it has its serious side. One of the ladies
shows them how to make a flag, — to cut the
staff, to sew the stuff and arrange the colors properly; the one who does the best work will carry
off the flag. While making it, they hear its history,
— that is to say, the principal facts in American

history.   The door is constantly opening and closing; mothers come to beg directions for cooking,
information and advice of every kind.   Some even-
ings there is music, — very simple little parties
no doubt, but they are made as pleasant as possible.
There are plenty of flowers and attempts at decoration; and none of it can make the invited guests
unhappy, since they share it all.   In the settlements for men, the capitalist, the student, and the
laborer meet as if by chance, on neutral ground,
on equal terms; and the results of this union may
be of great value in the future.

We must not suppose that young American girls
confine themselves to scientific and intellectual
charity.   They practise fashionable charity just
as French girls do.   I attended sales for various
charitable purposes, quite as brilliant as those
which take place in Paris, — one of them in particular, where all the articles on sale were Japanese,
and were sold by the most charming Boston damsels arrayed like Japanese, the decoration of the
stalls and the general arrangement being strictly
correct and very picturesque.   Neither good works
nor a passionate love of study deter from any
opportunity for pleasure.   It is wonderful to see
how fashionable society crowds the theatre when
the great comedian Joe Jefferson appears, or to

applaud the famous actors sent over by France!
The vast hall where weekly concerts are given
by an excellent orchestra, is always full. The
general air of absorption forbids a doubt as to the
sincerity of the interest taken by the audience in
these concerts, which last only about an hour and
a half, — a limit which might well be adopted
everywhere. Many young girls are good musicians; they are eager, as soon as may be, to set
off for Munich and Bayreuth. Those who draw,
study painting in France or Italy, — a pretext for
travelling. On their return they work without in-
termission, rivalling professional painters in their
ardor and their perseverance. "Nothing by halves"
seems to be the motto of all these tenacious, intelligent, and ambitious young persons.

The question which I read on the lips of my
readers is, "How can the strength of women,
herculean though it be, endure such an outlay of
activity; how can they bear these double, triple,
quadruple lives, led abreast and with full steam
on?" Remember the exciting, exhilarating influence of a dry climate, which puts quicksilver
into one's veins! Still, sometimes — nay, very
often indeed — the nervous strength thus put forth
gives way suddenly; the wings which bore them
up drop, and they fall exhausted. How common

are the symptoms of consumption, — the hectic
red spot on the cheek-bones, wan faces, pale lips,
and dark-circled eyes! Nervous disease is universal, and this is the reason why the "lessons in
relaxation" given by Miss Annie Payson Call are
so fashionable. America is probably the only
country in the world where the art of quiescence
has been subjected to principles of hygiene.

I have before me Miss Call's singular book,
"Power Through Repose." In it she states —
which I can readily believe — that a German doctor
who established himself in America was absolutely
dumfounded by the number and variety of nervous
disorders brought to him for treatment. At last
he announced the discovery of a new malady, which
he adorned with the name of "Americanitis." The
faculty strive against Americanitis in vain, special
private asylums increase constantly; rest cures are
ordered, as cold-water cures might be elsewhere.
Miss Call very judiciously invites attention to the
fact that the troubles produced by prolonged dis-
obedience to Nature's laws can be cured only by
a return to those despised laws. We must therefore learn — and her teachings hinge on this point
— to relax thoroughly in sleep; to avoid all nervous contraction in driving or riding; to think
calmly without the aid of any superfluous forces;

to look and listen without unnecessary tension ; to talk without excessive chatter; to manage the voice according to the principles of sound physilogy; not to sew with the nape of the neck; not to bring on cramp in writing, etc. The chapter which will give to French readers the most insight into the degree of excitement to which an American woman may attain, is that treating of diseased emotions, — the passion of pupils for their schoolmistress ; morbid attachments between young girls; artificial loves, which are merely love of emotion, not that of an individual ; in short, to translate it all by one expressive word which sums up the height of nervous over-excitement and entire loss of self-control, — "*dry drunkenness.*" As we read these pages, we feel with pleasure that France is the land of naturalness ; and we begin to appreciate that creature made up of good common-sense, "*Henriette,*" who always seemed to us exaggeratedly commonplace before we crossed the Atlantic. To exaggerate duty into pedantry and self-consciousness into obsession, these are faults of which Molière never dreamed. We have no expression in French equivalent to self-consciousness, which depicts a soul-state springing from Puritanism. Incessant examination of conscience is foreign to us. The Catholic religion accustoms

those who practise it to yield to guidance; the
result is, morality apart, a certain timid grace
and an amiable distrust of self.

Miss Call treats both soul and body, for she
tells us that a lady came to consult her in regard
to the cure of an excessive susceptibility; she ad-
vised her, whenever she felt wounded, to imagine
that her legs were heavy, which would produce
a muscular relaxation, a nervous liberation, and
relieve the tension caused by her excessive sensibility.   It seems that the prescription worked
wonders, this wholly outward process helping the
patient's mind to rise to a higher plane of philosophy.   We understand the following advice much
better: "Never resist a trouble; it is increased by
the effort which you make to overcome it.   The
body should be trained to obey the mind; the
mind should be trained to give to the body orders
worthy of obedience.   Avoid too great preoccu-
pation with self, insanity being possibly merely
egotism gone to seed.   The oftener you use the
word *I*, the greater your nervous trouble becomes.
Let us quietly accept all that Nature is constantly
ready to give us, and let us use it for the object
that she suggests to us, which is always the
truest and best; we shall thus live as the little
child lives, with the addition of wisdom."

The "serenity of a little child" is the ideal held up by Miss Call to her pupils. One of them told me that by teaching her repose, perfect relaxation of all her limbs, her teacher had put her into such condition that she could roll from top to bottom of the stairs without doing herself any harm. She invited me to assist at her lesson, and I gladly accepted. I went with her to Miss Call. I found her to be a young woman of calm and distinguished appearance, who in a few words and without the least charlatanry stated to me what she called her method, — not claiming that there was any new idea in it, but that it was merely a return to Nature. The restoration of the physical and moral equilibrium induced by the art of inaction may save the lives of many overwrought American women. It will also be introduced into France before long. Even the most coquettish of Parisians might be tempted by the costume which Miss Call wore, — silk tights, covered by a light silk tunic, leaving the arms and legs free. This Greek costume is not strictly necessary, — any ordinary gymnastic dress will do; but we were urged to pay careful heed to the play of the muscles which would be hidden in a different dress. Miss Call, stretched at full length on the floor, or standing in attitudes of perfect grace, did indeed produce the restful

effect of the abandonment of all effort and all voli-
tion. With closed eyes, she imagines herself as
heavy as lead, then slowly performs movements
enacted by each limb as if it were a part, as she
expresses it, of a bag of bones united by very
loose links. Great flexibility results. She has
adopted and enlarged the Delsarte system, which
is very widely known in America. But Delsarte
only practised the letter; she flatters. herself that
she has discovered the spirit. Certainly art should
benefit by her experiences; she believes that a
school of sincerity, in opposition to the dramatic
hysteria now too common, will be the result for
the theatre. Freedom, rhythm, equilibrium, such
are the qualities which she offers to teach by
a normal drill which, at the same time that it
strengthens the body, stimulates the brain. I
could only judge of the plastic part; and I must
confess that it was irreproachable. There may
be a closer connection than is at first apparent
between Miss Call's rest teaching and the precepts
of the new Christian Science, which also implies a
sort of quietism, a necessary reaction against the
untiring Puritan will.

Christian Science, which Mrs. J. T. Coolidge, Jr.,[1]

[1] "The Modern Expression of the Oldest Philosophy," by
Katharine Coolidge.

one of its adepts, offers us as the modern expression of the oldest philosophy, severely criticised though it be by some, bids fair to rival medicine in certain circles of New York and Boston. It is held in especial favor in Boston, so deeply imbued with transcendentalism, and ever mindful of Emerson's teaching, "Hitch your wagon to a star." It was to Boston, too, that the great preacher, the adored bishop, Phillips Brooks, addressed these noble words: "There is but one life, the life eternal." All this is perfectly in accord with the new or renascent science that there is not one principle for spiritual things and another for natural things, — the same principle acts throughout the universe. Matter is animated by divine life as is the spirit itself; products of the creative thought, we partake of its limitless vitality; our health, both moral and physical, depends upon this established current. The cure of physical evils is secondary; bodily health will follow when the soul is healed. So too Solomon refused to believe that God had ordered death, which entered into this world by the envious desire of the devil, and which threatens only those who are allied to him.

I sought out one of the distributers of Christian Science in her office: "Is it true, madam, that here in Boston and elsewhere more than one woman refuses to call in a physician when a child is born, because we should live without thought for the morrow, like the lily of the field?"

"It is a fact. Women who follow the teachings of Christian Science forget, at such times, as at all others, that they have a body. They discard all customary precautions; people are surprised to see them get up, walk out, and run what the vulgar call all sorts of risks, and yet suffer no bad results."

"But, after all, a broken leg requires setting. What should I do if I broke my leg?"

"You should say that it is not broken; that the pain is an illusion; and your leg will get well. A severe accident is far easier to cure than those chronic troubles which have become a bad mental habit. I hurt my arm not long since. I continued to use it, refusing to believe in any injury, and telling myself that with God's help all was well. Two days later I was entirely cured. Years ago I recovered my health, which the doctors declared irretrievably impaired, in this same way. I recovered it for my child, for many others."

"Can I be one of those privileged persons?"

"It all depends on the state of your soul. I am about to begin a course of lessons: you can join the class."

" Then you first advise those who suffer to persuade themselves that their suffering has no existence, and you fill them with your own conviction
until relief occurs? You magnetize them?"

" There is no magnetism about it; or at least
it is an involuntary magnetism, such as each of
us exerts on his brothers, and which represents
the increasing power to receive and give life. We
use neither hypnotism nor suggestion. We treat
the body through the soul."

" Religion commands us to submit to trials;
that is the way to suffer least, I grant you, for we
are thus spared the agony of impatience and revolt.
It seems to me that religion is all sufficient; but I
fancy that I should add a surgical operation to the
strength which it affords, if I had the misfortune
to require one."

This doctress of a new order smiled with indul-
gent pity at my blindness: "We cannot argue
until you have attended my lessons, and have
passed a slight examination."

" Of my conscience? Do you propose to feel
my spiritual pulse?"

"In a summary fashion and with discretion,
merely for the purpose of learning whether you
are in a fit state to be treated, and to help you to
attain to it."

She has a most honest aspect, mediumistic eyes, vague and dark-circled, with a sickly complexion, although she professes to be perfectly well since she has found the truth.   I place the price of my consultation on the mantelpiece and withdraw, thinking of a friend who, having been converted to this kind of spiritual cure, allowed the growth of an internal disease, of which she might have died had she not reluctantly called in earthly aid. "Because her faith was weak!" some may say. Others merely smile an obstinate smile, as did that handsome young woman who, only a few days after the birth of her child, followed me out, with nothing over her bare head and neck, to her door, and stood there on a freezing March day, defying the cold.

These instances will help to show the other side of the picture in Boston, — a picture moreover most interesting, painted at the same time with delicacy and vigor.   Infatuation is prevalent there; that is proverbial.   All America will tell you of Boston fads.   I witnessed two or three during my stay there; and if I did not collect more, it was probably for want of attention.   The most singular seemed to me that of which Mozoomdar, the Hindoo reformer, was the object.   Certainly, the Chicago Congress of Religions was a great thing.

That voluntary meeting of the ministers of all existing creeds, and the friendly exchange of ideas between them, bore a superb testimony to the tolerance of the age, and to the spirit of sincerity which prevails more and more as time goes on. Perhaps it may mark the era of a sort of spiritual unity; but it seems more difficult to admit that a unity of such recent date authorizes the utterance of Buddhist sermons from a Christian pulpit. However, I am less shocked by the comparisons made in Unity Church (Chicago) by Dharmapala, of Ceylon, between Christ and Buddha, — I am less shocked by this, I repeat, than by the pious heed paid by Boston ladies to the revelation of a new Christianity, an Oriental Christianity contrasting its glittering glory with the antiquated forms of our own.

The infatuation for Mozoomdar is an instance of the fad for persons; the infatuation for the " Intruder " and " Blind," [1] an example of a literary fad. The misuse of clubs is also a Boston fad. I think I have shown their good points; but the increase of clubs also increases coteries and sets. Are there not, as statistics show, two clubs for women lawyers, the Portia and the Pentagon? This is assuredly out of all proportion to the very small

[1] Maeterlinck.

number of women lawyers or law students.   Persons of one and the same profession risk becoming studied and artificial when they thus form a special class by themselves.   It is well sometimes to forget what we know and what we are.   Spontaneity, perfect simplicity are gifts too precious for a woman to risk their loss by excess of method and exclusiveness.   When we Frenchwomen wish to enjoy a book, we read it beside the fire, with no other end in view than our own pleasure, feeling no desire to repeat to each new-comer the famous question, "Have you read Baruch?" by way of winning converts.   In Boston, women who read combine together to criticise and discuss a book: at once a new club is formed, and given the name of some author or another.   The result is that in spite of all the praise I have bestowed on the conversation, it borrows from familiarity with clubs almost as many defects as good qualities ; it somewhat lacks lightness and spontaneity.   That rapid transit from one subject to another from which an unexpected witticism flashes, is rather avoided than sought.   Fluent speech is an art carried to a great height by some, both men and women, but rather in the form of a monologue.   Besides, the extreme politeness which is current, forbids anything even remotely resembling an interruption in con-

versation, even of the most intimate ; rather than
break in upon a neighbor's remarks, a return thrust
is often left unmade; and the formulas " I beg
your pardon ! " " Excuse me ! " recur oftener than
seems necessary. A little formality and artificiality
result. So, too, happy hits uttered anywhere are
gathered up, repeated, " put under glass," especially
when they emanate from those officially recognized
as wits. The latter could not be more petted at
the Hôtel de Rambouillet than they are by the
précieuses of Boston. We entreat those American
ladies who have no knowledge of this word, save
with the accompaniment of an injurious epithet,
kindly to forget their great favorite Coquelin in
Mascarille, and to remember that before they were
made ridiculous by Molière, the "*précieuses*" were
illustrious according to Corneille. The prudery,
affectation, and pedantry attributed to the degen-
erate imitators of that first circle of which virtue
was the soul, were but the middle-class exaggeration of very praiseworthy refinements and delicacies opposed by great ladies, who were also honest
women, to the common irregularities of manners
and speech. Like Boston, the Hôtel de Rambouillet represented a centre of intellectual culture;
and on looking back, we shall find in the one
almost all that is now current in the other, —

respect for virtuous restraint; cultivation of friendship; contempt for things which are gross and material; a voluntary forgetfulness of bodily wants and the conditions of old age; the subtilities of a conventional language bestowing pretty nicknames upon the initiated, etc. Just as the court and town were jealous of the Hôtel de Rambouillet, so great rival cities launch the arrows of envy at the Athens of America; which does not prevent the fact that it was from Boston in particular, and from New England in general, that the generous and noble impulse sprang which in France, about the beginning of the seventeenth century, spreading from the palace of Arthénice to all France, produced a general good breeding, politeness, and tact, whose very names were until then unknown.

III.

COLLEGES FOR WOMEN. — CO-EDUCATION. — UNIVERSITY EXTENSION.

COLLEGES FOR WOMEN.

AMONG the many theatrical posters which last winter proclaimed the performance throughout America of plays adapted from the French, and often retaining little of their origin, — side by side with " Champinol Malgré lui," converted into " The Other Man," and the colored silhouette of Fanny Davenport in Cleopatra (Sardou's Cleopatra), — I saw, by way of exception, something quite original. This poster represented a brother and sister dressed exactly alike except for the skirt, which prudently concealed on the young woman one of those combination suits so commonly worn in America in place of dainty linen, now out of fashion. The same waistcoat, the same hat, the same stick in the hand of each, the same field-glass slung across the shoulders, with the motto, which proceeding jovially from the lips of the one seems to compel the other to shrink back in horror: "Wherever you go, my dear Dick, I go too!" This is indeed the key to the situation.

The boys go to the university: the sisters insist
upon going there too. All existing educational
institutions, whether public or private, high schools
or academies, long since ceased to satisfy them ;
they are bent upon being prepared to enter every
career once reserved for men. I think I have
already stated that the great movements of the
contemporary life of women in America are shown
by the club and college, — association and culture.
The country begins to swarm with women doctors,
lawyers, and baccalaureates.

I was invited to a club of women graduates at
Boston. I have a vague recollection of having
shaken some hundreds of hands. That crowd of
young girls adorned with their college degrees was
truly imposing ; but I could not help thinking,
" What use is all this in the home?" I forgot that
America is a world in itself; that schools are
scattered thickly over its surface ; and that for
many years to come there will never be enough
teachers. All the fair damsels who talked to me
in the same breath of Vassar, Smith, Wellesley,
Harvard, and Bryn Mawr, where they took their
degrees, were as light-hearted as if they were not
overloaded with learning. The presence of men
could have added nothing to their inexhaustible
animation ; they were wholly sufficient unto them-

selves, munching cakes and sandwiches, and drinking a fantastic sort of tea in which lemon predominated. " What has become of the famous flirtation?" I asked a friend. She laughed and replied: "This is a different generation; there is no use trying to hide it. Flirtation decreases in proportion to the increase of culture. Many girls no longer care to marry; instead of conquests they aim at independence." Others assured me, on the contrary, that all the diplomas in the world would not prevent Nature from having her way, and that a university education was the best of all educations to fit a woman for the duties of life, whatever path she might elect to follow. I can readily believe the first part of this assertion; I am not quite so sure of the absolute truth of the second part. But I will let my readers decide for themselves, after a glance at a few colleges.

They are generally situated in the near neighborhood, and as it were under the wing, of the most famous universities. Thus in New York Barnard College is connected with Columbia; and so too, thanks to the Woman's Annex of Harvard, two hundred and sixty-three young girls, most highly privileged of all, are permitted to breathe, in the academic town without a parallel, that atmosphere of new Cambridge which has ripened so many splendid intellects and matured so many noble talents. Cambridge is new only in comparison with the old English Cambridge; for it was as far back as 1636 that a graduate of this latter university, John Harvard, created the centre of learning which bears his name. Time has therefore placed his mark upon the principal buildings, which are very venerable with their great yard shut in by gates of wrought iron and planted with century-old elms. One of these trees, known as the Washington Elm, bears an inscription in commemoration of the day when the great man for the first time drew his sword at the head of the American army, beneath its shade. The entire town seems sacred to study, history, and pious memories. I visited the homes of Lowell and Longfellow, still occupied by their families, and filled with books, busts, and pictures which are so many precious relics. In the Longfellow house, built in pure colonial style, Washington once lived.

Almost all these wooden houses have high gables or porches with columns. Those who show them to you name over most of the writers in whom New England takes such pride. The glories of their first greatness have faded, but the widows and daughters of those venerated dead are still there, surrounded by respect; they give their time, their care, their protection to the college for young girls, who make it a point of honor to pass the same examinations as the students of the University.

This college struck me as above all criticism for several reasons; the first of which is the moral guidance afforded it by Mrs. Agassiz, a person of great good sense and good taste, two qualities which, as we have often seen, rarely go hand in hand. The society in charge of the University education for women is made up, in Cambridge, of men and women of the highest distinction; the president, widow of the celebrated naturalist Louis Agassiz, seemed to me an American Maintenon ruling over a modern Saint-Cyr, which the pupil leaves provided not only with *bona-fide* diplomas, but also with solid principles and excellent manners. Four years spent in almost daily contact with such a character cannot fail to develop all that is best in each student. Another reason which makes the Harvard Annex unrivalled is the ever present influence of the great University, which lends it its own professors. The small number of students is also a real advantage, as is the system of boarding out, which distributes girls from a distance among families of the town. Dormitories of any kind are thus done away with.

Almost everywhere else they shocked me. Nothing could be more comfortable or more attractive than the rooms of boarding-school girls as I saw them in America; but the difference in their quarters cannot fail to produce envy and vanity, — unless as in the one college of Baltimore, the best rooms rightfully belong, not to the richest, but to the most meritorious. The custom of putting two girls together displeased me even more, whether a tiny parlor divided the two sleeping-rooms (I saw one girl receive her brother there, although he was not the brother of the other), or even when, as frequently happens, a single bed is shared by two. The Harvard Annex arrangement does away with all this.

One of the patronesses of the place — the eldest daughter of the author of " Evangeline " — took me over Fay House, which is the name of the building containing the class-rooms, laboratories, music-rooms, and lecture-halls. Everything is perfectly managed, without unnecessary luxury. The well-chosen library is particularly useful in connection with the reading-rooms, the University library being free to all students of the Annex.

Mrs. Agassiz has a tea every Wednesday. The students whom she gathers about her in motherly fashion owe to her the boon of education, so superior to that of instruction. The associate of her husband's great labors and long journeys, Mrs. Agassiz possesses a prestige which increases the value of her counsels. She agrees with Wordsworth and with Emerson. The former said of America that society there was provided with a superficial learning out of all proportion with the curb of moral culture. Emerson, who quotes this opinion, adds that to his thinking, schools may be of no benefit; that the education supplied by circumstances is often preferable to lessons properly so called; that the essential point is to avoid all falsity, to have courage to be true to one's self, to love that which is beautiful, to preserve one's independence and good temper, and to have the constant desire to add something to the well being of others. Most assuredly these sound precepts rule in the refined circle at Harvard; the women who graduate there are not only scholars, but pre-eminently "ladies," thanks to the sovereign influence of example and surroundings.

Another college of grand aspect, more lately founded (1884) in the suburbs of Philadelphia, is that of Bryn Mawr. Six separate buildings, of picturesque appearance, whose towers and gables peep through the trees, stand in a wooded region, surrounded by gardens and lawns. Some are used

as dwelling-houses, others for the various departments of study, managed according to the best
and newest methods.   The teachers, men and
women, live outside; no one lives within the walls
of the college but the students and their principal,
Miss M. Carey Thomas, who wears the impressive
title of dean with an infinite amount of kindly
authority.   Perhaps her perfect knowledge of the
French language, French literature, and of everything French may have had something to do with
it; but the type of the coming woman as described
by Tennyson, — free " to live and learn, and be
all that harms not distinctive womanhood," not
becoming " undeveloped man," not letting intellect
destroy all grace, — seems to me to be realized
in most peculiarly attractive fashion in Dean
Thomas.   Aided by young, active, zealous women,
whose great wealth obviates the necessity of all
sordid care, she plainly affords the noblest stimulus to a company of students whose number
barely exceeds one hundred and fifty.   It must
not be supposed that in America all degrees —
bestowed by the college itself, contrary to French
custom — are of equal value: the higher the rank
of the college, the more highly is the degree
esteemed.   A degree from Harvard, for instance,
opens every door to its possessor; and it is also

an inestimable distinction to have attended the
classical, scientific, or literary lectures at Bryn
Mawr. It is well known that there is no desire to
make a show, no frivolity, no shallowness, about
the teaching here, as may be the case elsewhere,
and that the woman who leaves Bryn Mawr a
master of arts, or even a doctor of philosophy, is
fully supplied with the stock in trade of a gowns-
man or a scholar. They are not only in earnest,
but very attractive, these young graduates, in
the black gown and square cap which they wear
within the college precincts, and which make them
look like Shakespeare's Portia. Their life seemed
to me delightful in every way. The freedom of
the country; the quiet desirable for undisturbed
work; the close proximity of a great city with
its artistic and other resources, which there is
nothing to prevent them from enjoying; four
months vacation, when they can travel; most
comfortable quarters; teachers picked and chosen;
every means, without a single exception, for de-
veloping moral as well as physical growth, — such
is their lot. In the vast gymnasium, I saw Portia
stripped of her doctor's robe, devoting herself to
exercises which prevent the spirit from over-mas-
tering the body. Loose Turkish trousers frankly
revealed the shapely leg; a shirt-waist with a

leather belt outlined a waist larger than is usually permitted by the American taste for slender figures; black-silk stockings and heelless shoes completed this pretty costume, and the whole testified that the danger of over-work had been successfully avoided.

The dean conducted me through the other parts of the establishment, containing class-rooms, studies, lecture-rooms, and bedrooms. In the main building, marble busts from the antique lined airy, sunny galleries. I was somewhat surprised to see the busts of Dante and Savonarola in the chapel, for I had been told that Bryn Mawr was founded by a Quaker; but in America, women who have grown up under the old régime are often astonished. For instance, the crowded condition of the laboratories proved a passion for biology which in Europe is very exceptional in young girls, but which is almost universal here. Each of these damsels was occupied in delicately torturing a frog or a lobster. Miss Thomas explained that their taste for chemistry and biology had recently been stimulated by the privilege at last granted to women of entering the Baltimore medical school on equal terms with men. Johns Hopkins, when he left his immense fortune to that city for the foundation of the University and hospital, also

wished to establish a medical school; but funds
were lacking. To make up the requisite amount,
a committee of ladies raised $111,731; then one
of the benefactors of Bryn Mawr, Miss Mary
Garrett, added $306,977, on condition that the
women students admitted should pass the same
examinations and be entitled to enter for all the
same prizes, dignities, and honors as their brothers.

"But," I said to Dean Thomas, admiring the
generosity of Miss Garrett, whom I afterwards
met, — and how modest, how simple, and how
sweet I found her, somewhat revolutionary though
she be in her ways! — " but all this swarm of girls
cannot mean to study medicine?"

"Certainly not," she answered; "but a little
biology will do them no harm, if it were only to
teach them many natural things in a scientific and
hence a healthy fashion."

I thought, without venturing to express my
thought, that in France, on the contrary, mothers
and teachers bend all their efforts to hiding certain natural things from their daughters until the
day when marriage throws an unexpected light
upon them; and I felt that I was, indeed, in another world.

This impression was strengthened yet further
when I saw the private apartments of the students.

All the work is done by colored women; the bedrooms and the little parlors are as prettily furnished as in the most elegant private house,
individual taste finding free vent here as elsewhere.
(In one college, not Bryn Mawr, I saw a room decorated with the flags of all nations, the bed being
skilfully hidden.)   There were plenty of tiny tea-
tables set round with be-ribboned rocking-chairs
well supplied with cushions; flowered curtains at
every window, plush curtains at the doors.   The
reception-room bore no likeness to the gloomy
parlors of Europe; the girls dance and sing in
it, and on certain fixed days give small parties.

"Visits are only allowed until ten in the evening," said my guide.

"Feminine visits, of course?"

"Oh, no! visits from relations or friends of both
sexes."

"What! with no supervision?"

Miss Thomas, who was much amused by my
absurd questions and my untutored wonder, showed
me that opposite the large parlor, on the other
side of the hall, was the private sitting-room of
the lady in charge of that building.   Neither of
the rooms had a door, — nothing but open arch-
ways and loose curtains.   This is the case with
almost all reception-rooms in American houses,

the general use of furnaces making this possible. Flirtation, in any case, is not veiled in mystery.

" There are very few formal rules at Bryn Mawr," says Miss Thomas. "The students go to Philadelphia without asking leave save out of deference; they never abuse this privilege, it being to their own interest not to miss lectures, because they come to college to work."

" Will France ever have a Harvard Annex or a Bryn Mawr?" I ask myself this question as the evening train bears me back to Philadelphia; and I feel that we are terribly in the background. But I am seized with the fear that once started, we may move a little too quickly along paths, which, patterned after foreign roads, without regard to our native obstacles, are not those best suited to our temperament and our powers.

My ambition does not, for instance, lead me to wish for a French Wellesley, with its seven hundred students. This college seems to me decidedly too large; it made me forcibly aware of the danger which threatens the United States, — too much culture in all ranks of society, since culture thus spread broadcast cannot be very profound. Moreover, we cannot but wonder what effect is produced on girls, most of whom will be obliged to earn their own living, by these four years spent in the palace of the Ideal, this intermediate space between the mediocrity of the past and the cruelties of the struggle for existence which awaits them. For the name of " palace," or at least of " castle," is excellently suited to Wellesley, as it mirrors its noble architecture in an enchanting lake in the midst of a park of some four hundred and fifty acres. For the modest sum of $350, sometimes lessened by gifts or by loans from an active Aid Society, Wellesley students enjoy not only every means for acquiring a degree, or for perfecting themselves without further object in literature, art, and science, but the pleasures of the material life are also lavished upon them. They find comfortable shelter and the best of fare in the six pretty cottages, each under the charge of a matron, which are scattered around the main buildings, — College Hall, the fine Art School, and the Music School. Lake Waban is theirs to row on, to hold regattas on in summer, and to skate on in winter; then they are but fifteen miles from Boston, which implies a constant series of interesting visits. On the day when I received such cordial hospitality at Wellesley, Richard W. Gilder, the poet, lectured on President Lincoln as an orator, and other eminent guests sat down to a luncheon simply but substantially served, — the President, Miss Helen

Shafer, doing the honors, while a company of the scholars waited on the table. The founder of Wellesley, H. F. Durant, desired that this should be done, requesting that each student should give daily at least forty-five minutes to some part of the domestic labor in order to glorify those useful tasks and to prevent the claims of caste.

The beauty of the place charmed us all. As far as the snow permitted, and beneath a brilliant sun which made it sparkle brightly, we traversed the vast park, which combines everything, — the beauties of both art and nature, hills, woods, meadows, running water. Some one ventured an enthusiastic comparison between this college and that of the princess who in the English poem gathers about her all the young girls of her father's states, with the intention of freeing the sex to which she belongs. The similitude was the more just, since Wellesley College, while it does not forbid the entrance of men on pain of death, is the only college which is wholly in the hands of women, who are alone allowed to serve as members of the faculty, although there are men serving on the board of administration. Mr. Durant and his wife, who survives him, have always asserted very decided opinions upon this point. The history of the foundation of the college (1875) is both singular and pathetic.

A famous lawyer, heart-broken at the death of
his only child, abruptly left the bar, in the prime
of life and at the height of his triumph, to devote
his life to religious and philanthropic work. He
was inspired to insure to the whole body of the
young girls of his native land the benefits of an
education which would fit them for any career;
and in the month of September, 1871, the corner-
stone of the main building, College Hall, was laid,
side by side with a Bible.

College Hall is a fine structure, in brick and
stone, in the shape of a double Latin cross. It is
entered from a vast hall paved with marble, full of
green foliage plants, in the centre of which the staircase rises, lighted from above in the Italian fashion,
with balustrades and galleries on each floor. Pictures and statues abound: the statue of Harriet
Martineau, by Miss Whitney, seems pointing the
way, at the very threshold of the house, to the
woman logicians, economists, and reformers of
the future. The large parlor for the use of the
faculty is elegantly adorned. Another parlor is
dedicated to the memory of Elizabeth Browning,
apparently as to the purest and loftiest of women
of genius; it contains every known portrait and
bust of the author of "Aurora Leigh," as well as
autograph manuscript of her husband.

The magnificent library numbers more than forty thousand volumes, thanks to the generosity of Professor Horsford, of Cambridge. The students have free access to this library, which is arranged with matchless system and regard for individual wants. Numerous Reviews, both English and foreign, may be found on special tables; the same thing is also true of all the other colleges. I should be in danger of constant repetition if I were to name over the various clubs and societies to be found in each of them, — the members of these societies, which bear names significant of their object (Phi Sigma, Zeta Alpha, Agora, etc.), desiring to stimulate literary studies, or to rouse an intelligent interest in the questions of the day, or to devote themselves to music under the inspiration of Beethoven, and so on. As a matter of course, there is always a Shakespeare Society, and also a Christian Association to guide religious ardor towards social questions. The theatre too has its devotees on the plea of amusement: as we visited the various floors of the college by the help of the elevator, we came across a laughing troop of young actresses, prettily arrayed for the dress rehearsal of a play.

In the park there is a Conservatory of Music containing forty pianos, an organ, and a recitation room for the use of choral classes. Concerts overflow into the chapel, always a matter of scandal to visitors from Catholic countries: they should remember that to Protestants the church retains its sacred character during religious service, after which it becomes a place to be used for any purpose.

The School of Fine Arts, built in Greek style, crowns a hill. We can scarcely say, in spite of the gifts which it has received, that its galleries are lined with masterpieces; but it is very well arranged with respect to lecture halls and studios, where drawing, painting, architecture, and designing are taught. I see among the collections a case filled with fine old embroideries, and I venture a question which receives the brief reply: " The students leave the needle to the professional schools."

A full-length portrait of Mrs. Alice Freeman Palmer, in the Art Gallery, is an agreeable reminder of the second president of Wellesley, who was universally considered as a skilful organizer. Miss Shafer, before she succeeded Mrs. Palmer in office, was a most successful teacher of mathematics. Up to the date of her untimely death, which occurred soon after my visit to Wellesley, I am told that she held the standard of classic and scientific studies firmly aloft, whenever it was a question of granting a diploma, although she allowed great liberty in regard to what are known as electives. Let us consult the ever eloquent statistics upon this head. Seven thousand girls, in the space of some twenty years, have spent more or less time in study at Wellesley. Associations exist among them, from one end of the United States to the other, enabling us to count up those who have turned their literary or scientific acquire-ments to advantage; and it seems that their number is great. But university degrees were won by only eight hundred and forty-seven students; of this number five hundred are teachers and professors, twenty or more are missionaries, some dozen are doctors, and about as many journalists. One hundred of them have clung to family life.

I had no opportunity to visit Vassar College, — which, if I am not mistaken, is oldest of all, — nor Smith, founded ten years later, about the same time as Wellesley, and about as large as that. Among establishments of recent date, the College of Baltimore, opened in 1888 under the patronage of the Methodist Episcopal Church, seemed to me destined to the largest measure of success. The charming capital of Maryland, where it is situated, affords many advantages, — a very mild climate, cultivated society, the neighborhood of a univer-sity, abundant libraries, art galleries like that of

Mr. Walters, which is open to the public on stated days and combines a large number of the finest masterpieces of the modern French school, and lastly the Conservatory of Music, due with so many other gifts to the munificence of George Peabody. The construction of the Woman's College also testifies to that private generosity so commonly found in America. The Rev. John Goucher erected the impressive hall in Roman style, where laboratories occupy an entire floor, the rest being devoted to classes, assembly rooms, collections of minerals, botanical and paleontological specimens, etc. Mr. B. F. Bennett, in memory of his wife, added the massive edifice in the same style devoted to physical culture, and containing a swimming-bath and gymnasium constructed after Swedish methods, which bid fair to oust German methods throughout America. The teachers in charge of the gymnasium are from the Royal Institute at Stockholm, and the famous Zander apparatus is used to correct by proper movements any weakness or deformity in the pupil. Once a year the progress made in lung capacity and muscular power is measured.

Two separate buildings afford the students something very like family life. I notice, when I go through them, that the dining-rooms as well as the kitchens are situated on the top floor, to avoid all odors; elevators running constantly prevent any inconvenience which might otherwise arise from this plan. The girls eat at small tables seating eight. I talk with some of them, pretty as all Baltimore women are reputed to be, and possessed of a vivacity and grace which are decidedly Southern. There is no shadow in them of that somewhat haughty pedantry which I sometimes observed in the North. Then, too, they have greater skill in turning a compliment. I have reached the South; I already feel the affinities which exist between this part of America and France.

In spite of the religious influences which reigned over the foundation of the college, there is almost as much personal liberty here as anywhere else. While there is a rule forbidding the students to attend theatres or balls, drink wine, or play cards, the girls are permitted to give a monthly party under the direction of the lady in charge of the housekeeping, and each girl is allowed to invite one or more friends.

Food and lodging cost two hundred dollars a year; tuition, one hundred dollars, not including accomplishments, with ten dollars extra for the use of laboratory apparatus. Of course, only a college very richly endowed could give so much for so small a price. The beautiful Methodist

Episcopal Church in Baltimore serves as the college chapel, there being a private passage between the church and Goucher Hall. The campanile is a more or less faithful copy of San Vitale; and amid all these structures of Lombard architecture in rough-hewn granite, it is indeed fine, solid, and severe of aspect. A preparatory school, known as the Latin School, thrives close by the college, under the same rule.

At Baltimore I also found the excellent preparatory school of Bryn Mawr, which takes pupils as young as eight or nine, and carries them to the very door of the college. I got there just before a talk on hygiene, and I admired the way in which practice is combined with theory. These young day-scholars have their swimming-school; they take lessons in fencing, and practise archery. Their vacations are longer than is usual in France. I am therefore struck by their healthy looks, which in the future some will lose by too much brain-work or too much social dissipation. They also seem to me, I must say, less well bred than European school-girls of the same age. English travellers in America have always noted the tiresome exuberance of the children, accustomed to rank as important personages. This remark proves that English children are timid and strictly governed; but it is certain that the inevitable individuality does not wait many years before it asserts itself in the small American, and more particularly in the small American girl. But let us return to the universities towards which this rising generation will eagerly tend.

There are now in the United States (since the triumph of the Union, the South has taken a large part in the educational movement) one hundred and seventy-nine colleges for women, in the sense which the English language attributes to that word "college," which has nothing in common with French establishments of secondary instruction, — one hundred and seventy-nine colleges conferring degrees. These colleges number 24,851 students and 2,299 professors, — 577 of whom are men, and 1,648 are women.[1] The predominance of women does not lower the standard, if I am to believe the best judges. They are of the opinion that there is in feminine teaching greater method, which makes up for the power of improvisation, the species of personal genius which insure the superiority of masculine teachers. Moreover, there is no spirit of unfriendly rivalry between the professors of the two sexes, — a thing to be explained briefly thus:

[1] Not all have the title of "professor;" there are also "teachers" or "instructors."

the field is not crowded; the sum total just quoted
proves this.   Many college professors are obliged
to add to their already overwhelming work the
care of preparatory classes, and the crowd of
aspirants for the higher studies is always growing.

This passionate attack upon the tree of knowledge fills Frenchwomen with humiliation when
they chance to witness it.   How many of us know
enough to enter college?   But we make it up in
regard to history.   American women, and many
American men too, seemed to me very ill-ac-
quainted with history, as soon as they stepped
aside from that of their own country and of England, which is directly connected with it.   But our
self-love need not take fire.   I am disposed to believe that the very consciousness of our lack of
knowledge is in its way a kind of superiority.   A
distinguished professor, talking with me of these
matters, pointed this out to me: "Yes, the education of our women includes many more subjects
than yours, — it includes far too many; it is like
an unfinished sketch, without shadow or details.
They are certainly better at mathematics, — there
is no room for doubting that, — and they learn the
dead languages; but I doubt whether in most cases
they derive much benefit from that, except to succeed in passing examinations.   Here we are unfor-

tunately compelled to put ourselves within reach
of a certain mediocrity sure of itself, and certain
that there is nothing beyond its comprehension.
An American woman without over-weening pre-
tensions is the first among women; but nowadays
we should have to sift them well to find one who
does not aspire to everything."

It is very rarely, I admit, that an American
expresses himself thus freely in regard to his
learned fellow-countrywomen. At most they will
say, in speaking of this rage for culture: " It is a
moment of transition in some ways unfavorable to
family life; but who knows whether, after the inevitable tentative essays, we shall not benefit by
it?   Who knows whether the result may not be
a woman far more perfect than any in the past?"

One can never guess just what lurks behind the
humorous half smile of an American; these words
which I also caught seemed, however, to imply a
regret and a threat.   "Everything moves quickly
with women.   Fifteen years ago, colleges for
women were attacked as vigorously as their right
to vote is now.   Well, their colleges work wonder-
fully well after all. Let us only hope that they
will not go too far, for their own sake; they may
end by being so strong and so well armed that
we shall have no further cause to show ourselves

chivalric in regard to them, since your French
politeness awards us that flattering epithet. And
the day that we cease to protect them, they will
undoubtedly see that although they have more
university degrees and political rights, they are
far worse off than before."

These are very mild criticisms; but I would not
for the world reveal the names of those from whose
mouths they fell, not wishing those rash men to be
rent by furies. We may truly say of America that
" it is forbidden there to strike a woman even
with a flower." When I expressed my surprise,
on two or three occasions, at the liberty that
prevails in these colleges, men, without exception,
always answered dryly that at the age the students
had reached — sixteen or seventeen at least — before entering upon college life, they ought to know
how to behave. The watchfulness, the restrictions
thought needful in the convents and boarding-
schools of our Old World would be a gratuitous
insult in the colleges of the New World. The
blameless conduct which distinguishes the woman
student in her class-room she retains in all the
details of her life; to doubt this would be to doubt
the benefits of the whole system of education which
governs America, and which is based upon self-
respect. In no country is there a stronger feel-

ing of fellowship among women; in no country are individual friendships nobler and more devoted. So I am told, and I believe it; I often had proof of it. It is certainly to be desired that the same solidarity might exist between Frenchwomen of all ranks in society. But there is another side to the picture, and it is sometimes impossible to avoid seeing it.

CO-EDUCATION. — GALESBURG, ILLINOIS.

We have yet to make acquaintance with those colleges where the system of co-education prevails, — a system stranger to foreign eyes than aught else. These colleges are to be found almost exclusively in the West. A man of high rank in the department of Public Education spoke to me in terms of the utmost praise of the results obtained from first to last under this system of co-education, which has lately been the subject of such hot discussion in France, where, of course, it could not possibly be used without a complete change of customs and manners. Mr. William T. Harris, Commissioner of Education at Washington (he will pardon me for using his name), believes that the fact of living together from earliest childhood, in the kindergarten and primary school, renders boys and girls less susceptible to the attraction of

sex. He has noticed that the rivalry established between them accustoms the girls, who often out-rank the boys, to set little or no value upon block-
. heads, even if they be handsome. Moreover, they may have brothers in college, who protect them; and the greater part of their comrades have a genuinely fraternal feeling for them, — their com-radeship having always existed, and the change from childhood to youth having come upon them almost unconsciously. An important fact asserted by Mr. Harris is that though some cases of miscon-duct may have accidentally occurred in the schools for girls, they are unknown in the mixed schools. The former apparently admit of far greater freedom ; the latter require from their girl pupils a reserve only equalled by the respectful timidity of the other sex, accustomed as boys are not elsewhere to take the intellectual worth of women into account.

It is impossible for me to have any personal opinion on these questions; I merely discovered that our European prejudices are shared in the great Eastern cities. At Chicago, I saw scarcely more than the outside of the gorgeous university founded under the inspiration of the Baptist Church; and it seemed to me too new to be altogether vener-able as yet, thoroughly provided though it may be with everything which money can buy. Perhaps the story of a week or two passed in a prairie college, that at Galesburg, Illinois, will show my readers, better than anything else I might say, the system of co-education in its most interesting form. The aspect of the college is inseparable in my memory from that of the little town and its inhabitants. I will therefore set down some fragments from the journal whose pages I then filled every night.

It is about five hours' journey from Chicago to Galesburg. I am the guest of one of the college professors, who, like all Americans, is loyal to the principle, " The friends of our friends are our friends too." Rich or poor, they invite you, on this excuse, to share their family life as easily as we invite a friend to dinner.

The house is a plain wooden one; it stands at the extreme edge of the town. The fence built about it opens on the street which leads to the college, — a road planted with rock-maples, and with plank sidewalks on either side. Three or four rooms on the ground floor, with as many above them, — no more; but this modest interior at the first glance suggests ideas of order, scrupulous neatness, and studious retirement. On the dining-room wall hangs the Lord's Prayer in ornamental script. The library is adorned with books which overflow into every room in the house. There are no mirrors in the tiny parlor, only the simplest furniture, a few good engravings, family photographs, and flowers; a rare dignity prevails. This is the setting for one of the noblest and most vigorous figures that I ever saw, — that of an old man robust as any youth, an unselfish scholar, whose well-filled life has been consecrated from beginning to end, in spite of the counsels of ambition, to this college; he may well be called one of its pillars. Beside him is his wife, delicate and shy, whose face still bears traces of one of those ethereal beauties such as we find, exquisitely engraved, in English " books of beauty." By the way that the household is conducted, with the aid of but one small black girl, I see that there are good housekeepers in the West. The professor holds to old-fashioned ways: nowhere else did I find so perfect an instance of the Puritan family, as I had imagined it. The husband and father is still master here, and a tyrannical master too; the wife submits with a grace and sweetness not especially American; the daughter is respectful and reserved. And yet she has a high degree of culture, as proved by her diplomas; she teaches in the college, and has undertaken, with girl friends, what her parents never

did, — a journey to Europe, after which her life of
retirement and toil seemed no harder to her than
before. Everything (bread, clothes, etc.) is made in
the house; of course the mother must lend a hand.
The fare is plain, but abundant; temperance is not
only preached but literally practised in regard to
fermented liquor.   The father pronounces a bene-
diction upon every meal.

The history of Knox College at Galesburg, as it
was told to me, has some unique features. A band
of patriotic and Christian pioneers laid its foundations.   It was their avowed purpose to create a
college which should furnish well-trained recruits
for the evangelical ministry, and make women
worthy teachers of the future generation. January
7, 1836, a meeting was held at Whitesborough (New
York State); it was voted to raise the sum of
twenty thousand dollars, the price paid for fifteen
thousand acres of land, the sale of which represented the first gift to the college; and in the
spring of the same year the colonists, headed by
the Rev. George Gale, the prime mover in the
scheme and leader of the colony to which he gave
his name, turned their steps towards the prairie.
In the autumn thirty families, forming a homo-
geneous nucleus springing from the Pilgrim fathers
of old, had already built rude cabins on the spot

where the city was to rise later on. In 1837 a charter was obtained for the establishment of the college, and at the end of 1838 the college opened with forty students. There are now six hundred. The present buildings were not finished until 1837; and during the same year a seminary, where girls are lodged, was built. Since then a gymnasium and an observatory have been constructed, and in 1890 the corner-stone of the structure known as Alumni Hall was laid by President Harrison, with words which linger in the memories of all: " Once more we dedicate this institution, already sacred to truth, purity, loyalty, and love of God." The college has had intelligent and zealous benefactors. One of them, Mr. Hitchcock, gave the college such part of his property as his wife might not require for her own use; and Mrs. Hitchcock, with equal generosity, gave up what the law allowed her, in order that her husband's wishes might be carried out, and herself took up her abode in a cottage at Galesburg.

A MORNING VISIT TO ALUMNI HALL.

The building, of Roman architecture, in brick and red sandstone, is very handsome. The auditorium, daily used as chapel, holds nearly a thousand persons. Morning prayer calls together the entire college, and the professors take turns in reading the Bible, which is followed by a brief address. I hear the professor of English literature speak upon " Comparisons," *à propos* of the mote and the beam of the Scriptures. This custom does not exist in the State universities; it seems to me to contribute largely to the moral atmosphere of Galesburg.

We visit the town, which is charming with its shady avenues and its verdant boulevards. It covers a vast extent, trees and gardens occupying much space. Green trees surround the principal buildings. There are a few mercantile streets, but they are quietly busy, as befits a town where trade is only a secondary matter, which has never cared for anything but religion and learning. The elegant quarter is filled with very pretty middle-class houses, mostly of painted wood, but of every architectural style. Lawns encircle them; they seem indeed to be scattered over a meadow. The entire town is scrupulously neat, with the hideous sidewalks which everywhere in America, in the streets, parks, and outside the houses, enable the foot-passenger to avoid mud or dust, according to the season. Some streets are paved with improved bricks. The interiors, seen through bow-windows adorned with flowers, are pleasantly homelike.

We visit a suburb made up of tiny houses painted in bright colors, well varnished, like brand-new toys ; this is the Swedish quarter. These worthy people form a very important part of the population, and soon grow rich by their industrious habits.

There is an immense parade ground for three companies of soldiers commanded by an officer of the United States army, sent here to teach military science and tactics. Military drill is obligatory, each student being required to provide a uniform.

There are many churches, representing every Protestant sect, and also, in the form of a minute fraction, Catholic worship. The college was founded through the efforts and sacrifices of the Congregationalist and Presbyterian churches ; their influence is therefore dominant in the board of government. But there is no narrowness ; a genuine Christian spirit is alone required as the fundamental and indispensable basis of education at Knox. Students attend their respective churches on Sunday.

I attend the class in Latin, taught by a young girl with expressive and resolute features, who seems to exert a great influence over her scholars. She has almost as many boys as girls in her class. Although it is not required by any rule, the two sexes are divided, and are seated on separate sides

of the room.   The girls are usually more advanced ;
they smile somewhat mischievously at every mistake made by the boys, who seem equally glad to
catch them at fault.   There is no coquetry on the
one hand, no gallantry on the other.   I notice the
sunburnt hue, the rustic air of many of the students,
— grown men ; their pleasant faces express both
energy and openness.   I am told that they come
from remote parts of the West, and that before
entering college they earned the requisite amount
of money by manual labor.   The keeper of a large
shop said to me as we travelled in company: "I
once travelled all over this part of the country on
foot, with a bale of goods on my back, in my
vacation ; and I did that year after year, to pay
my way through college.   They used to call me
the honest little pedler."   And it was plain that
this was one of the most agreeable things that had
ever been said of him, although he had since won
great success.   Many of the pupils at Knox College
are of the same substantial stuff.   These backward
fellows sometimes prove themselves possessed of
superior and truly original talents.   Several were
pointed out to me who, during the Chicago exhibition, without any false modesty, spent their ten
weeks' vacation as waiters in various restaurants at
the Fair, or in pushing wheeled chairs.   And now

they are here, deep in the Æneid. The merry, kindly influence of the girls upon this set of country lads is of the happiest sort. The spur of rivalry urges them on; they are ashamed to be outrun by their more delicate mates; and, moreover, feminine goodness almost unconsciously refines them. If the professor who teaches chemistry with rare spirit and clearness did not choose the girls as the subject of his questions during my visit, in order to show a stranger (very incapable of judging) how much they know, I think the boys might possibly have the advantage here. But I have preconceived notions on this head, which the aptitudes of American women apparently prove to be mistaken ones.

Am invited to several houses in the town, where I find the best of company, — women simple, and at the same time well informed, talking on all subjects, and asking intelligent questions. Evidently contact with the college is a constant stimulus, and the society of the professors a precious resource. Some have travelled; but they are not possessed by that feverish desire for change which I have remarked elsewhere; nor is there any trace of pretence or affectation, — which is restful. The diversity of religious denominations in this little town, which is so devout as a whole, is singular.

At a certain lunch I met half-a-dozen ladies, all very intimate, although belonging to different churches. Opposite me sat a Baptist, and at my side a pleasant Universalist, whose religion I like, because it allows her to be as sure of my eternal salvation as of her own.   Universalists condemn no one.

I continue to visit college classes taught by women.   They hold only the secondary rank of instructors.   Knox College maintains the supremacy of its professors with jealous care, priding itself on possessing a body of teachers which could not easily be matched throughout the West.   The French lessons attract me.   Just now the pupils are reading, translating, and expounding Victor Hugo's plays.   They are at work on " Hernani," and nothing could be funnier than the accent given to those impassioned verses, those Spanish titles, over which they stammer and bungle.   But they understand enough, I fancy, to consider Hernani quite mad.   I afford them genuine satisfaction by telling them that even in France such sentiments seem somewhat exaggerated.   Among those who are evidently on the rack during the ticklish scene of the portraits, are some of those handsome, sunburned, firm, and frank youths of whom I have already spoken, — young giants come hither from distant farms, who have deserted the

ploughshare for their books. One of them hesi-
tatingly addresses me, and asks with eager curiosity
if it be really true that the admiration of the
French for so great a man as Napoleon is dying
out. Emboldened by my answer, he next expresses his conviction, shared by many others,
that an obscure soldier was shot in place of Marshal
Ney, and that the latter took refuge in America.
The questions of the girls refer to far more personal
matters. What they want to know is whether the
education of women in France makes any progress;
if French girls are still shut up in convents; if it
is true that there is no such thing as co-education
in France!

A very pleasing young woman is the professor
of elocution and the Delsarte system, which teaches
the art of graceful gestures and attitudes, readily
assumed by the girls, but imitated with most amusing painstaking awkwardness by the boys. One
morning I drop into a class where I find five or six
men gathered about the desk of a young woman.
She is teaching contemporary and political history
and the Constitution of the United States. She
seems prettily embarrassed by her task, and leads
the conversation with the tact of an intelligent
hostess, encouraging the discussion of serious
subjects rather than herself taking part in it.

Supper at the Seminary. — The students who do not belong to the town almost all live here. Around the table are the professors, men and women, with a few guests. The dining-room in which we are, opens into another much larger room, where the pupils are seated in groups of six or eight at little tables. The principal presides. A small number of students come from outside to take their meals with the girls. After supper, in the fine, large parlor, all the pupils are presented to me, one after the other. There is a long procession of very varied types, often most pleasant to look upon. They come from all parts of the United States, — from Kansas, Colorado, California, Texas, and I know not where. I am told not only their names, but also their native State. Several come from Utah, from Salt Lake City. I shudder, imagining myself in the presence of Mormons; and they laugh, explaining that their parents are " Gentiles." Moreover, the Mormons have lately renounced polygamy, which involved them in too many difficulties. The evening ends with a concert. The orchestra is ably conducted. Fragments from " Carmen " are played in my honor.

I have promised to spend the afternoon at a large farm in the neighborhood. In America all country estates are known as "farms." In his excess of hospitality the farmer proprietor comes for me himself in his buggy. Borne along by two stout horses, we roll across the prairie, breathing in a soft and velvety air which, before the wintry blasts appear, forms a part of the exquisite season so well named "Indian summer." The landscape with its monotony is new to me, who never saw the steppes. It is the vast prairie, rolling in little short waves, and broken only by fences, — the sometimes straight and sometimes zigzag barriers which throughout America divide the fields and restrain the cattle. The silvery color assumed with age by the wood of which they are made harmonizes admirably with the brownish tint of the soil. The corn has been gathered in; only the stalks and the long leaves collected in shocks for the cattle remain. Here and there, where trees have been felled, the stumps are rotting in strange long rows, no one taking the trouble to root them up. These stumps bristling through the freshly tilled land are a common feature of the American landscape.

The farmhouse to which we are bent stands in the midst of three thousand acres, partly cultivated and partly prairie. We stop before a wooden house, built after the usual plan, with a stoop,

the movable step leading up to it, and the indispensable sidewalks.   The mistress of the mansion
comes forward to meet us.   Nothing in her reception betrays a shadow of provincial ceremony.
She leads us into a parlor furnished in black hair-
cloth, and the conversation soon turns upon interesting topics.   We are told that two days earlier
the farm would have afforded us a curious sight.
Herders from the Mormon country stopped there
with eighty thousand sheep, which they were driving to the Chicago market.   The bleating troop
besieged the house with the noise of an invading
army.   Now we shall see only the offspring of the
farm, — horses and cows, scattered over the vast
extent.

About one o'clock dinner is served; a purely
American dinner, — soup made of canned oysters,
roast meats, stewed corn, raw celery, rhubarb pie,
native grapes which taste like black currants,
hickory-nuts, and tea or coffee by way of bever-
age.   Two young girls wait on the table; they are
introduced to me as the daughters of the house.
They must needs assist in the work of the household during one of those domestic crises so frequent in the West, and to some extent everywhere.
The refusal of Irish and Swedish servants to eat at
the same table with negroes complicates the diffi-

culty still more.   Self-help is therefore obligatory.
The tasks accomplished by these young girls do
not however prevent them from going to school
in town every day; they drive themselves in their
own little carriage.   As we chat, I discover that
the life of a farmer's wife is somewhat hard in
America, where the clearings are so far apart and
on so vast a scale that there are no small matters
to be looked after.   There are no neighbors and
no amusements.   But in winter, at Galesburg, the
farmer's wife finds compensations.   She belongs to
a literary club; all the ladies are members of it;
accordingly they can do a great deal of reading in
summer on the subjects proposed for future meetings.   I inquire as to these subjects, and they tell me
of some of them, — troubadours and trouvères (the
Romance tongues are in high favor in the United
States, and many persons who cannot speak French
fluently go into ecstasies over our old Provençal
literature); the influence of the salon in the seventeenth century; Frenchwomen in politics; origin
of Greek art, etc.   Such interest in things of the
Old World is hardly credible in a prairie village;
for a town of eighteen thousand inhabitants is
scarcely more than a village in the United States.
But this particular village most assuredly has a
soul superior in quality to that of many big cities.

One of the party tells us of a recent visit to the Indian Territory, which lies between Missouri and Texas. The government having bought the land from the Indians, granted it to the first comers. The result was that an army of riders appeared from all the region round about. The narrator showed us instantaneous photographs which give an idea of the mad race, favored by the flat country, and of the victory won at headlong speed. We also saw the victor resting, seated on the ground, in the fresh enjoyment of his estate, — a land-owner for the first time in his life, but half dead with hunger and fatigue; then the city in process of formation, — scattered tents; the beginning of traffic, represented by a shop in a board shanty. But to encounter equal things one need not go very far from Illinois where we are. On this very spot Indian sepulchres have been found, skeletons resting among the highest branches of the trees. A discussion followed in regard to the Indians, whom some consider capable of learning the arts of civilization, particularly agriculture, while others declare them to be apt at everything but work.

The laborers employed on the farm are all Swedes, — honest and industrious therefore. I see their tiny houses scattered among the trees

and on the plain.   They cut, reap, and thresh the
grain, with the help of the most perfect machines.
There is nothing picturesque about it.   The bronzed
cheek of the master proves that he has overlooked
them closely, and that his own task is no easy one.
He laughs cheerfully at ready-made phrases in
regard to the delights of a rural life, and at all the
beautiful lines penned by poets ancient and modern on the subject of the fancied joys of the rustic.
"Virgil never visited America," he concludes by
saying.   The ladies talk of Paris, where the two
fair Hebes who poured our tea at table are to finish
their education.   I dare not tell them that they
will hardly find as many resources there as in Galesburg.   We are not invited to take that look around
the establishment which is inevitable in Europe.
Western country regions are not yet provided with
smooth footpaths; people walk from necessity upon
roads leading to a practical end.   Our little grassy
paths, only meant to be trodden by long generations of leisurely people, will come later.

About sunset I again enter the buggy, from
whose high seat I witness one of those sunsets
which kindle a splendid conflagration in the sky
overarching the limitless prairie.   The youngest
daughter of my host, a lovely child of nine, springs
upon a horse, regardless of her short skirts, not

even delaying for a hat, and escorts us to the turn
in the road, where she stays.   I gaze back at the
figure of the tiny Amazon with floating hair, as it
stands out black against the purple background;
and I feel that sad, sweet emotion which has more
than once stolen over me during my long journey
full of new faces and new scenes, — the feeling
that I am breaking a bond but just formed; that
I am leaving too soon people or things which I
came near loving, which I shall never again see.

Another expedition as far as Knoxville, in a more
beautiful landscape, the vast sea of the prairie being
more rolling.   My companions pointed out to me
that wherever there are woods a creek flows under
the fresh foliage, which accompanies and reveals
its windings.   At this autumn season the creeks
are mere brooks, but in winter they overflow the
very roads.   Sometimes the eternal fence is re-
placed by hedges, where the osage orange hangs
like a great ball of green wool, which will soon
turn yellow.   Among the groups of oak and maple,
now and again, we see a painted wooden house, and
a farm; then we go long distances without seeing
anything but a solitary barn by the roadside, or
again a sort of large lonely cabin behind its fence.
I shall see similar ones everywhere at two-mile intervals.   They are schools supported by neigh-

boring farmers, who, remote from cities, have no other way to educate their children.

Knoxville, a small town already dead, although it is not much more than fifty years old, persists in retaining an air of importance with the two or three pretentious edifices, with triangular fronts, which adorn its chief square. One of them formerly sheltered the court, which has since been transferred to Galesburg. There was a lively struggle between the two towns, and the inhabitants of Galesburg will tell you why it ended in their favor. Knoxville was originally peopled by Southerners, while its rival was founded by Puritans from the North; if we are to believe them, it was the inevitable triumph of all the good qualities to be found in a mighty race. Perhaps the fact that it is situated on the main line of two of the largest railroads in the West, the Burlington and the Santa Fé, making it easily accessible from all parts of the country, may have had somewhat to do with inclining the scale in favor of Galesburg. Be this as it may, Knoxville slumbers in the shade of her big trees, white and clean, with broad streets lined with trees, and a magnificent school for boys established by the Episcopal Church. A short distance off, in the country, is a no less monumental Institute for girls, under the same patronage. St.

Mary's (that is its name) would have reminded
me of a European convent, if an accident had not
brought me there at the recreation hour which follows luncheon.   All the girls were on the road, on
foot or in carriages, driving themselves, munching
apples, all· very merry, very elegant, and certainly
far more worldly than the pupils of the mixed college.   Not far distant is an almshouse, which looks
much more like a handsome hotel than a home for
paupers.   All ages are assembled there, and most
humane concessions are made to family life, for I
was told of a widow who had just been taken in
with her three little children.

We cross the railroad track, there being nothing
to forbid access to those who desire to be run over,
and we return to Galesburg by delightful roads
skirting the woods.   A buggy passes ours, containing a young man and a girl.   I ask the professor
who is with me if they are engaged to be married.
" They may become so," he replies, " but not
necessarily."   And I see that this stern man un-
derstands and approves that things should be as
they are.   Upon this point he is of the same opinion as all the fathers of families whom I met in New
York and elsewhere, — they think it perfectly natural that their daughters should ride horseback,
should go and come escorted by a young man

friend. But I do not know whether his tolerance would equal that of many others if his own family should attempt to put his theory into practice.

I have made an interesting discovery. The friends who show me such cordial hospitality are descended from Barbara Heck, the mother of Methodism in the New World; at the same time I learn how the establishment of this sect in America is connected with the conquests of Louis XIV. The Germans driven from the Palatinate sought protection under the English flag in Marlborough's lines, and grants of land were made to them in Ireland; they were eminently worthy people, much inclined to religious ideas. The Wesleyan doctrine of the witness of the spirit fell upon their souls, well prepared to receive it. They set sail from Limerick in 1760, not to avoid poverty, but to go in search of a promised land, according to the words of the Bible that those who " do business in great waters, these see the works of the Lord and His wonders in the deep." Among them was a young woman quite recently married, who was their guide and support throughout the vicissitudes of exile. Landing in New York, they gradually lost their first ardor. Barbara put them to shame for this lapse. Supported by her old German Bible, she dared everything. For instance, a love of gambling having seized the little colony, she entered the gaming-house, took possession of the cards, burned them on the spot, and converted the gamblers. The influence which she exerted over her people was that of a second Deborah. The Methodists had no church; she resolved to build one. Service was arranged, thanks to her, in the house of her cousin, Philip Embury, whom she electrified by her example. She worked all the week to earn her daily bread, and then distributed spiritual food to an ever-increasing multitude. There are three Methodist Churches in New York, not counting negro churches; and one of them stands on the site of Philip Embury's humble home. When Barbara Heck died, in Canada, at a very advanced age, after sowing her religious beliefs in that region, she declared that she had never, for twenty-four hours at a time, lost the evidence of acceptance with God from the age of eighteen years, the date of what she called her conversion, because the Spirit had not spoken to her until then. I tell Barbara's great-grandchildren, who are Congregationalists, how surprised I am that they should have forsaken the church founded by such an ancestress. They reply that it is much easier than we think to change from one Protestant sect to another, the differences between them being chiefly in the form of government. They are all of one communion, except the Baptists, who hold themselves apart.

The longer I stay in Galesburg, the more strongly it reminds me of some little German university town. There is the same simplicity, the same worship of learning and its representatives, the same patriarchal customs. The German spirit, shown by a general knowledge of the language, prevails here as in many other American cities, — the result of immigration, of the more or less lengthy sojourn made by the professors in Germany, and also of that distinction which attaches to the victorious party seen from afar. The majority do not speak French, although some look back with delight to a brief visit to Paris.

The presence of the professors, their mothers and wives, lends a grave charm, which I enjoy immensely, to one or two very small evening parties. The military instructor, whose uniform adds a gay note to that gray and black symphony, is more worldly than his colleagues. My questions all bear upon the system of co-education, with its advantages and its dangers. The president's pretty wife says: "My husband and I can say nothing against it, because we met and fell in love at college." My host's oldest daughter was married in the same way, after winning all her degrees. Yes, many matches are made in college. Is that an evil (they ask)? Would it be better to meet in society, in the midst of mere trifles? Do not people learn to know one another far better, and under more interesting aspects, when they study together for several years?

"But these marriages are premature."

"Not at all; they do not take place until the man has made a place for himself. The constancy of the pair is often put to a prolonged test."

"And does not love distract you from your work?"

This very French suggestion caused a smile. An American does not think of a woman until he has first thought of his important duties, and also of his means for supporting that woman. The example of the youthful president of Knox, who has recently succeeded a man universally esteemed, whose age obliged him to seek some relative repose, — the brilliant, almost unique, instance of a position of such importance attained at the age of thirty, — proves that matrimonial engagements made at college do not hinder great efforts and great success. I am asked if I have seen anything, either in the college or in the town, which suggested any of the disadvantages to which I refer. Certainly not. Well, there is nothing. The atmosphere of Knox is healthy and serene. Each individual respects the dignity of every other individual without the intervention of strict rules. New-comers soon see this; they understand what is expected of them, and they very naturally fall in with it.

I hear of the distinguished men who have graduated from Knox College. Ministers of the Gospel and professors predominate, — that is to say, the people who care least for the material pleasures of this world, who care most for the life of the spirit.

My conclusion, after hearing everything, is that the system would not succeed in a larger city, where a ceaseless moral guard could not be kept, where the religious influences would be less direct, where there would be temptations or even distractions. The still primitive manners of the West allow of the realization of that which anywhere else would be a Utopia. There are many other colleges founded on the same basis as that of Knox; and this testifies to a rectitude of soul, to fresh and robust virtues to which it seems to me the more completely Europeanized America of the East does not do full justice. There are prejudices on both sides, in the West as well as in the East, for lack of better acquaintance. Did not an uncompromising native of the prairies write me the other day: "Come again and stay longer. As my mother says to her visitors, 'Come again and bring your knitting!' What pleased me in your first visit was your determination to see the *people* of America and not its snobs. The true American is not to be found in drawing-rooms. It is only in the little towns, the villages, in the country that the democratic ways which characterize him still exist. How long will this resist the rising tide of money and its insolent privileges? I cannot say ; but it exists in our homestead, where I spend the summer, eating at the same table with the hired girl, and where the gardener calls me by my Christian name, my Top name, as Walt Whitman would say."

The man who says this, a talented writer, is admirably adapted to endure the harsh influences of a farm in Wisconsin. I am more eclectic than he. The wild perfumes of the prairie do not prevent me from appreciating certain New York and Boston drawing-rooms; but I have often been shocked at the wilful ignorance which Americans who had crossed the ocean a dozen times, profess for those parts of their country which are still new, just as if the treasures of the future were not buried there. I left Galesburg with regret; I return to it from afar; I still think of it with sympathy and respect. It would be a great pleasure for me to go again and "take my knitting," as I was invited to do in the frank parlance of the West.

UNIVERSITY EXTENSION. — CHAUTAUQUA.

Before leaving the subject of colleges, I feel that I must needs say a few words about a popular movement in the direction of higher culture which is as beneficial to women as to men. University extension means the various methods afforded to all classes of people for acquiring a more extended education than can be found in schools. Or rather the university taken in this sense is, according to Professor Moulton's excellent expression, the exact antithesis of the school, — the school being obligatory, governed by an unchanging discipline, while the university, thrown open to the masses, is the education of adults; a voluntary and un-limited form of education, applied to the entire extent of life.

England originated these methods, which con-sist of lectures, weekly exercises, questions and answers, all ending with an examination, which enables the pupil to receive a certificate in regard to the studies prosecuted. The movement began as early as 1850, but the University of Cambridge did not fully organize it until some twenty years later. Oxford followed the example, and a society was formed in London for the extension of a mode of teaching successful beyond all that could have been hoped. It has since been carried into Scotland and Ireland, and was at last transmitted to the United States, beginning in that most enlightened city, Baltimore.

Dr. Herbert Adams, — who kindly took me over Johns Hopkins University, where I was received by President Gilman with a courtesy which I can never forget, — Dr. Adams, the professor of history, told me how, during the winter of 1887–1888, the young people of the city met together once a fortnight to hear lectures on the history of the nineteenth century. Another set of lectures upon the advance in manual labor was afterwards given for the benefit of the industrial centres which abound about Baltimore. But it was soon seen that this kind of instruction could not be given to any special class, whether they were workmen or not, but must be open to all, without regard to profession.

Such was the spirit which governed the classes

subsequently formed with the assistance of those Young Men's Christian Associations which exist in every city. The movement grew steadily stronger, until now all colleges lend their professors to help it on. To see the colossal proportions which a grain of mustard seed borrowed from the Old World may assume in America, we have only to glance at the Chautauqua School.

At the very time when, as I have already shown, Boston was preparing to naturalize English methods in a limited circle (1873), a great idea was springing to life in the mind of the Methodist bishop, J. H. Vincent. It was first revealed to the world at a summer school held on the shores of Lake Chautauqua (N. Y.) for the purpose of teaching the Bible. This sort of Sunday School held in the woods was the starting point of a popular university, which, by virtue of the charter granted by the State of New York, may confer degrees. The camping ground has become a sort of summer resort, to which the Erie Railroad and the Lake steamboats annually bring thousands of students. They find there hotels, museums, gymnasiums, public halls, a " Hall of Philosophy," a " Palestine Park," amusements of all kinds, — excursions, regattas, fireworks, — a little too loudly advertised and vaunted perhaps; but if it be true that the

end justifies the means, we must forgive Bishop
Vincent for everything.

Convinced that life is a school, with educational
influences at work from the cradle to the tomb,
the bishop desires to assist these influences by
keeping in sight individual capacity and surrounding circumstances. All knowledge leads us to
God, provided we ascribe it to Him. It is a universal duty of every age to aspire to develop the
mind. The man who, even in his old age, feels
the need of guidance of this sort has as much right
to it as his juniors; and a just reward should be
given to his efforts. The Chautauqua School
therefore adds to its work by correspondence,
an annual reunion at which there are classes and
examinations which lead to the conferring of a
sort of diploma. This meeting opens on the first
Tuesday in August, and lasts several weeks, on
a spot which might attract a crowd merely by its
picturesque beauty. Unfortunately, I was not
there at the time when the multitude starting from
the temple and from Jerusalem, or stepping from the
boats which traverse the lake, go up through
the sacred grove of St. Paul to the hall which
forms the centre of the magic circle to take part
in those exercises known by the name of the
" Round Table," which always begin with a prayer

and end with hymns. We will let Mr. John Vincent speak for himself: [1] —

" Every chair is occupied long before the hour appointed ; benches are brought forward, shawls spread on the ground, and many stand. It is a fine sight to see that mass of human beings crowding about the snowy edifice, amid green trees, with the lake hard by, and the rays of the setting sun playing on the quivering leaves, upon all those luminous faces. We unconsciously think, as we listen, of another lake, upon whose shores the Word was given to men of noble purpose."

In Bishop Vincent there is something of the apostle, and also of the seer who lives in the contemplation of an almost celestial Chautauqua, whither — thanks to electricity — coming generations shall be borne in the twinkling of an eye to behold the perfected wonders of the telephone, the phonograph, the microphone, etc. ; where the changing hues of luminous fountains shall mingle with the living waters of the lake ; where all tongues shall be taught by natural methods, visitors being free to travel at will through the German, French, and Italian quarters, as well as through other foreign regions which shall make

[1] The Chautauqua Movement, by John H. Vincent. Chautauqua Press, Boston.

of this University a world. So, too, all may enter
one common church, sacred to the spirit of charity
which brings all Christian sects together, and where
the liturgies of all ages will find a place, without
prejudice to spontaneous products. Dr. Vincent's
hopes, as we see, do not stop at a "local and
literal Chautauqua;" they include a " Chautauqua
of ideas and inspirations," so lofty that it is scarcely
of the earth. This artless and generous enthusi-
ast might well vie with Peter the Hermit; and it
is indeed a modern crusade that he preaches.
Chautauqua now has branches in all directions;
also summer residences whose various advantages
are indiscriminately boasted, — culture, religion,
music, walks, and restaurants. The impulse given
by Bishop Vincent is in reality the same which once
produced revivals, spiritual awakenings; and it
took place under the same Methodist influences,
although they now extend to all churches as well
as to all branches of human knowledge. The
American taste for everything that is sketchy,
merely hinted, so long as the design is huge, well
set off by puffs and highly colored, finds free
vent among the two hundred thousand Chautau-
quans who boast that they have followers in India,
Japan, Africa, and the Pacific islands. But it cannot be denied that this encampment of a whole

nation round about knowledge, vulgarized to excess though it be, has some elements of greatness. Whatever we may think of a certain abuse of the flourish of trumpets, we must salute the good man who said: " It is the mission of the true reformer, the true patriot, the true Christian, to offer learning and liberty, literature, art, and religious life, to all people, everywhere."

IV.

A WOMAN'S PRISON. — HOMES AND CLUBS FOR
WORKING WOMEN. — DOMESTIC LIFE. — IN-
DUSTRIAL SCHOOLS. — AGRICULTURAL IN-
STITUTE AT HAMPTON : NEGROES AND
NEGRESSES.

A WOMAN'S PRISON : SHERBORN.

I FEEL that all I have said of Boston would be
incomplete if I failed to add my impressions of
Sherborn Prison, conducted and managed solely
by women. Mrs. Ellen Johnson has proved for
the last ten years — she proves every day — what
patience and determination can make of the most
degraded of all beings. She has charge of the
financial part of the prison as well as the moral
and material direction. Everything passes through
her hands; and she fully justifies this system of
autocracy. Her model reformatory has the advantage of being in the heart of the country,
although not more than an hour's journey from
Boston. The surrounding market-gardens completely isolate it. The country through which we
travelled, still attractive in spite of its shroud of
snow, was undulating and shut in by wooded
hills. Yonder huge building of red brick, with

15

large out-houses which seem to indicate a great farm, is the prison, — a prison without walls or fences. In front of it lies a garden belonging to the smaller of the two main buildings, which are separate, although quite close together. This is the home of the directress; the other contains the prisoners, whose number varies from three to four hundred. None of them are sentenced for life; the term of imprisonment does not often exceed five years. But there are some exceptions; for we find murderers at Sherborn, and infanticides and incendiaries, as well as mere vagabonds and incorrigible drunkards. The last class is unfortunately most common of all.

Mrs. Johnson is a tall, stout woman, about fifty-five years old, whose open, benevolent countenance expresses the calmest energy. She has a very striking look of moral and physical health. Goodness is apparent in every line of her round full face; but we see at the first glance that there is nothing sentimental about this goodness, and that it is not mixed with weakness. She leans upon no outside authority, and although the prison has, of course, inspectors, they give her free sway, appreciating her thorough competency. She knows each one of her pensioners, and her powers of observation have reached the highest point. A bunch of slender keys hangs at her girdle; she walks before us, followed by her little dog, whose bounds and gambols seem almost out of place, so suggestive of liberty are they.　From a pretty room full of flowers we pass into the large, light corridors of the prison, and the Superintendent shows us her kingdom, and answers all our questions.

Yes, she lives alone in her part of the house, absolutely alone, served by prisoners.　We saw one of them, the young girl who opened the door for us.　She wore the prison dress, but the red rosette fastened to her waist shows that her conduct is irreproachable.　This little bit of ribbon, one of Mrs. Johnson's happy ideas, has done great service.　Every distinction gained helps to raise the moral standard of these poor women, and she never lets the slightest effort go unrewarded, — not merely strict obedience to rules, but private, individual advance, more important than all the rest. She is not content with passive submission; she believes that the conscience of the ignorant and fallen can only be aroused by trusting them to themselves up to a certain point.　The prison system is wholly based on this theory.　Thus the prison dress at first sight is alike for all, — a blue and white checked gingham.　But look again; that check, according as it is larger or smaller, according as it has one, two, three, or four bars, shows that its wearer belongs to one or the other of four divisions. After the first weeks of solitary trial, the new-comer is put with her companions; and there she has an opportunity to struggle incessantly to obtain better food, a little freedom, various privileges. To do this, she must rise from the last grade but one to the higher grades. It may also happen that she falls to the last. We shall see, if we follow Mrs. Johnson, what this means.

It seems impossible to imagine anything neater, more shining, and better waxed than Sherborn prison. Air and light enter freely everywhere; we smell no bad odors, and indeed no odors of any sort, anywhere; not a grain of dust, bright coppers, scoured and whitewashed walls, stairs so beautifully kept that they look like new. We seem to be moving in the pure atmosphere of some picture of a Dutch interior. This cleanliness becomes almost excessive and distressing in the kitchen. Is it possible that such well-scrubbed tables, such carefully scoured utensils are ever used? And how is it that no emanations rise from the three huge kettles which are all on the boil? Mrs. Johnson lifts the covers: one holds cocoa-shells, another oat-meal, the third a delusive imitation of coffee, which in all three cases is equivalent to hot water. This is the usual fare. Very little meat is used, and but once a day, in a semblance of broth. To make amends for this, the women can have an almost unlimited amount of bread cut in thin slices, as is the American custom, and very white. Clearly, the strong soups and coarse bread used in Europe are more nutritious.

" This is enough," observes Mrs. Johnson. " If they were better fed, they would be harder to manage ; and our sanitary condition is all that we could wish for."

Sufficient or not, this meagre fare is very neatly served. And here we note the stress laid upon decent and respectable habits by all who have Anglo-Saxon blood in their veins. The punishment for the worst women is to eat out of cracked or broken dishes. This is part of the ingenious system of the four grades which our visit to the four dining-halls shows us. In the dining-hall for the lowest class everything is of the coarsest description. Every article of the crockery and tableware is damaged; the food also is made up from the leavings of the other tables. The corresponding cells are the least convenient in the prison; closed merely by a curtain, they open on a passage-way which is strictly guarded. Mrs. Johnson told us with an air of satisfaction that there were

but nine of these outcast prisoners.   They were
formerly far more numerous; but by good conduct
several have gradually risen to the first division,
which gives them certain delicacies, choice dishes,
tea once a week, and a little butter.   In the four
divisions the regularity of the setting of the table
is a masterpiece of exactness.   No fork projects
beyond another; the eye travels along two lines
which seem as if drawn by plummet and rule,
and the table manners must be equally perfect,
— hands and feet placed according to rule, and
not one moment of forgetfulness.   The success
of attempts made at the famous Elmira reformatory (New York State), where certain criminals
were gradually made morally straight by being
physically straightened, compelled to walk upright,
to look their fellow-men in the face, to give up
those visible bad habits which are but the reflection of hidden faults, — the final success of these
experiments, I say, seems to have been the subject
of deep thought with Mrs. Johnson.   She believes
that a proper bearing should be regarded as a
symptom of good omen, indicating the return of a
certain self-control; and she consequently punishes
the slightest lack of decorum.   But her punishments are not very severe.   The delinquent is sent
to a special cell, barer than the others, with a grated

door; for serious faults there is the dungeon, — a dark closet under ground, with no bed but the floor, and no food but bread and water. There were formerly several of these dungeons, but Mrs. Johnson has been able to do away with all but one, and it has scarcely been used for a year or two. She has often gone into it herself with some poor wretch made hysterical through fear, to advise her gently, to persuade her to beg pardon; or, if she were obstinate, to bring her warm coverings to protect her from the cold night air. Except in these extraordinary cases, the punishments and rewards are always the same, — the going up or down from one division to another. The first division thus constitutes a select circle. We meet a young woman as we pass through the corridors, decorated with the red ribbon, a book under her arm. The Superintendent taps her affectionately on the shoulder. "This is a very good girl," she says. "She would not lose that ribbon for anything in the world. Would you?" and she called her by her Christian name. "For if a woman once deserves to lose it, she can never get it back again, no matter what she may do," explains Mrs. Johnson turning to us.

We visit the ironing-rooms, the sewing-room, and the mending-room. Every prisoner leaves the prison with a trade by which she can, if she choose, earn an honest living. Besides, those who cannot read are obliged to attend a class in reading and writing every evening; the others may attend a class in history and geography if they wish. They have a library, and the book most in demand seems to be that work of compassion, "Uncle Tom's Cabin." They are allowed to take out books during their hours of recess, which are very brief and carefully guarded. Everything that keeps them from talking together is considered wholesome. In a half hour's conversation they go back to the past; they exchange too many confidences, they get excited, the improvement steadily made for weeks or months may all be lost. Mrs. Johnson hopes to do away with this fatal half hour, which is only conceded to the too feminine need for talking; she is searching for some way of filling it with amusements which require silence, such as music, or visits from kind souls from the outside world. But it is a very delicate matter to select these visitors: they must not be easily impressed, disposed to emotion, nor prying persons who like to listen to all sorts of tales. Mrs. Johnson refuses to hear the story of any of the prisoners; she does not allow herself this too facile form of interest, but takes them

up at the point where she finds them. Yielding
to morbid sensibility does no good to these un-
balanced natures. The faces which I saw in the
work-rooms reminded me of those of the patients
at the Salpêtrière. They sit with their backs to the
door, so that their attention may not be diverted,
and they hardly turn their heads when we enter.
But I notice their weak features, their hollow eyes,
their foolish or brutal countenances. Their hair is
neatly dressed in braids; but the only pretty face
is the sullen one of a very young mulatto girl.
The long rows of backs presented to me express a
peculiar and significant laxity. These work-rooms,
admirably ventilated, and heated by steam like the
rest of the house, are as free as the other apartments from the heavy, disagreeable odors of work-
rooms generally, even when they are not prison
work-rooms. The prisoners are compelled to ob-
serve the strictest neatness. Each cell contains
the necessary utensils for washing, with a little bed,
a chair, a Bible, and the rules fastened to the wall;
very often a rosary. In fact, four-fifths of the inmates of Sherborn are Catholics (Irishwomen), and
they are the only ones who retain any religion;
some of them are very pious, and partake of the
communion regularly every Sunday in the chapel,
where the two forms of worship are celebrated in

turn.   Protestants who have fallen thus far, believe in nothing.   Does not this difference afford room for thought?   They have the same Scriptures, the same examples of the Canaanite and the publican, of Mary Magdalen and the thief; yet the one despair, and the others feel undying confidence. Protestantism is assuredly the proud religion of those who have never sinned.

The decoration of the chapel, where a Protestant service follows the Mass, seems meant for Catholics.   Above the platform, in front of which the congregation sit, is a figure of the Virgin between two other figures, — on one side Christ saying to the woman taken in adultery, " Go, and sin no more; " on the other, the infant Jesus in the manger, surrounded by poor wretches, who fill a sort of cavern, in the back of which a light shines, with the inscription, " A little child shall lead you."

A lady who lives near often plays the organ, and enchants these impressionable creatures by thus speaking to them in the language which they can best understand, — that which touches at the same time the senses and the soul.   In many ways, this young woman, rich and artistic, is Mrs. Johnson's active assistant.   Other charitable persons have helped to beautify the amusement room, which is only opened on certain festal days, and is adorned with conservatory plants and flowers, among which tame birds flutter. There are all sorts of games and pictures. A play is sometimes acted by the prisoners, who make their costumes with the matron's help. Some enter into this with great spirit, and, indeed, intelligence. But the thing which amuses them more than anything else is work in the fields, to which continuous good conduct entitles them. In squads and in silence they mow, or dig potatoes. Nothing is healthier, more strengthening than contact with the earth. So Mrs. Johnson strives to find places on farms not only for those women who are set free, but also for those she thinks she can answer for before their time is up. It is so hard to get " help " that Sherborn has more applications than it can fill. Sent into remote country districts where they live in daily relations with simple, honest people who have no other servants, these sinners gradually become accustomed to family life, to good habits; some have so far reformed as wholly to forget their shameful past.

" I have only," says Mrs. Johnson, " to succeed in inspiring them with some very lively taste, some passion, which may be directed into a proper channel. You have no idea how useful animals have been to me in this way. I have set them to raising silk-worms; I occupy them in the stable; once I gave out little chickens by way of reward. Nobody would ever believe how much affection they lavished upon those tiny chicks, which grew up with them, which were their very own. But my little calves accomplished the greatest miracle. We had a hardened woman here, who, when she had finished her term, went straight back to a house of ill-fame as the only place where she was happy. She returned here, after fresh crimes, determined to resume her vile profession for the third time, as soon as she could. I then tried to interest her in two new-born calves. I sent her out to play with them. She made friends with them; finally devoted herself to the dairy which we had just established, and in this way found her place. She is now a farm servant, and contented with her lot."

Mrs. Johnson prides herself on her dairy, and on the excellent butter which the women make. Part of the milk is used for the children in the house. Of course, this active reformer, who is so well aware of what can be accomplished by giving people something to love, has not failed to try the power of maternal love; it would be the strongest of all forces if women did not sometimes sink below the level of the very beasts.

We pass through a small room where two girls

are preparing nursing bottles and pap. "This," says Mrs. Johnson, "is the children's kitchen. We have some fifteen children, all born in the prison. The rules only allow us to keep them until they are eighteen months old; but I manage to forget their exact age." In spite of repeated disappointments, she still continues to hope that association with these poor babies will help their mothers to return to a sense of duty. Alas! to most of them, the child is merely the embarrassing evidence of sin: they do not love it. It was found necessary to withdraw the permission originally given them to keep their children with them at night. The babies were abused, beaten, the victims of violent and animal impulses.

The nursery is a fine large room on the first floor, looking out over the country on all four sides. We find there fourteen children of various ages, some carried in the arms of prisoners, who are not their mothers; others are in charge of a matron. I never saw anything sadder: they are as silent as if already crushed by the weight of rules and regulations, and their poor puny faces express a vague sense of shame and disgrace. No playthings are allowed them lest they should hand them from one to another; for many of these off-springs of drunkenness and vice have inherited contagious diseases. They are only too fortunate when they are not morally rotten almost before they are born! Mrs. Johnson tells us in an undertone of one little monster whose precocious depravity was so indomitable that she was forced to send it away.

"What became of it?"

She turns away as she answers me: "I never asked; it was taken to the almshouse."

It is terrible to think what the future of this unclean waif may be; how little protection and pity it can expect elsewhere, when it failed to interest even a Mrs. Johnson, at the age which is supposed to be the age of innocence! This brief and horrible history pursues me like a nightmare.

In summer, the children are taken out to walk, but in winter they never leave the house, having no warm clothes; their little gingham gowns are the prison uniform. When I see them, they wear their sad winter aspect, — prisoners with no amusements, still too young to learn anything, and neglected by their mothers who rarely ask for them. It seems as if a European mother would still feel for her children even at the last degree of degradation; the fall here, when it occurs, is apparently more complete. Mrs. Johnson struggles against all those evil instincts; she chooses her assistants carefully, and only deputes to them a comparative degree of authority. Everything depends upon her, from the most serious questions to the smallest details.

We are taken to the storerooms, piled up with boots and shoes, dry goods, etc. The Superintendent attends personally to all applications from the prisoners, and supplies them with her own hands. " If one of the women needs shoes," she says, " I am here to give them to her, and we talk. I offer her a glass of milk; I win her confidence. I never let an opportunity pass to get nearer to them." The gospel spirit is still the same: the sick must be touched, to heal them.

Not one man lives at Sherborn. The matrons are discreet and well-mannered persons; the doctor, whom we met in the pharmacy, is an intelligent woman, who seems inspired by a true spirit of devotion. The chaplain is Miss Ettie Lee.

Doors still continued to open and close for us, — doors which have nothing repelling about them, but which are of iron all the same. We have completed our round. Mrs. Johnson draws our attention to the fact that there is an entire avoidance of the system of close, narrow courtyards, high walls, and visible precautions against an attempt at escape or communication with the outside world. Every window looks out on the fields or the yard, but no passer-by is allowed to cross the prison bounds. Quiet, solitude, separation from the outside world, the healthy influences of Nature, — these are Mrs. Johnson's assistants. When she took charge of the Sherborn penitentiary, stern measures were often required; there were revolts, threats, and stabbings. Nothing of the kind exists now. A recent incident shows the measure of her influence. As she was on her way to the chapel one evening, the prisoners following her down a long passage-way, the electric light suddenly went out. It was a moment of agony for Mrs. Johnson, — alone, in utter darkness, with more than three hundred women, some of whom might be fired with evil intentions. But, without losing her head, she ordered them to halt in silence, and to keep their position. " The light will come back directly," she said. But no, the light does not come back; two, three, four minutes pass, which seem like a century. When at last the corridor is again lighted, the women were still in their places; not one had moved.

Mrs. Johnson tells this story with the quiet pride of a general doing justice to the discipline of his troops, in the comfortable, flowery little parlor to which we return after visiting the prison. The young prisoner in her gown, with its fourfold plaid,

protected by a maid's white apron, handed tea.
Mrs. Johnson talked cheerfully.   But my mind still
dwelt on the stern asceticism of a life voluntarily
spent in such surroundings.   I was full of admiration and respect for this woman, who, left a child-
less widow, has made for herself a large family of
criminals, outcasts, and repentant sinners.

HOMES AND CLUBS FOR WORKING-WOMEN.

Miss Grace Dodge's family, taking the word in
the same broad and sublime sense, — Miss Dodge's
family is made up of working-girls.   Her Association has more than a thousand members, who are
all gathered together at the annual meetings, to
which some hundreds of others who are interested in
the work are also invited.   Miss Dodge belongs to
the city of New York, and holds a high rank on
the board of Public Instruction, being a commissioner of education.   She established her Association of Working-Girls' Societies in 1884, in a bare
room on Tenth Avenue.   At first she gathered
around her, without requiring any fee, about a dozen
girls who spent their days behind the counter in
a shop, or in working for factories.   At the end of
a month there were sixty of them, and they agreed
to pay twenty-five cents a week apiece.   The

same Society now has a large house for which it pays one hundred and twenty-five dollars a month, sub-letting part of it for eighty-five dollars, which reduces the Society's rent to forty dollars, amply covered by the fees for membership. As in other organizations, of which I shall find occasion to speak, there are classes in cooking, embroidery, and sewing. There are also weekly practical talks, which have been one of Miss Dodge's great means of usefulness. The subjects are very characteristic of American ways; for instance: " Men friends; " " How to find a husband; " " How to make money and how to save it." One delightful detail is the fact that a sort of confraternity to help those who are poorer than themselves, was founded by the members of the Association as soon as it became thriving.

I am told that the spirit of imitation rapidly does away in these clubs with that extreme coarseness but too frequent among American women of the laboring class, although they may have attended the public schools, — a fresh proof that instruction and education are very different things. It is much to be regretted that all New York shop-girls do not belong to these clubs. The mere word to " serve " no doubt to them implies some degree of shame. The more ordinary the shop, the more aggressive the sense of social equality seems to be among the employees. Now the club has this advantage: it brings persons employed in first-class houses into contact with poor beginners. Workers in jute, silk, paper, carpet, and cigarette manufactories are associated with dressmakers and girls from the best shops; and thus the contagious effect of example is soon seen.

The object of the Association founded by Miss Dodge is to unite, protect, and strengthen the interests of the various societies of working-girls, modelled after the first one, by collecting them in a single union. Closely connected with this group is the house on the north shore of Long Island, known as Holiday House. A generous lady placed this large house, with the fields and woods surrounding it, at the service of working-women whose health made it necessary for them to take a rest. For three dollars a week a girl may enjoy all the benefits of Holiday House and all the delights of the country. The clubs pay the travelling expenses; they all have fresh-air funds, and also arrange for this with the Working-Girls' Vacation Society, made up of rich girls, who, while they traverse the world for their own pleasure, do not forget that other young girls, tied down to their work, have neither opportunity nor means for travelling. They therefore busy themselves in finding out country farms where their less fortunate friends may find good fare at a low price; they obtain railway tickets at reduced rates for those whose families live at a distance; and they get free excursion tickets for those who have but a very short leave of absence. The frantic luxury of New York is atoned for by an equal outlay of intelligent philanthropy. For instance, when I saw the Vanderbilt palaces on Fifth Avenue, I said to myself that this superlatively rich family were fully entitled to house themselves royally, having contributed to the physical welfare and social progress of so many. Christian Associations for young men and young women have no more generous patrons.

The buildings of the Young Men's Christian Association, with the surrounding fields devoted to athletic sports, stand on the southwest corner of Twenty-third Street. There seven thousand young men, who, were it not for this refuge, would probably pass their evening in a far less wholesome way, find books, lectures, classes, games, every opportunity for instruction and honest amusement. Countless visitors may be added to the regular members. The latter scarcely pay a third of the expenses, which mount up to one hundred thousand dollars a year; friends do the rest. So too in Fifteenth Street, passers-by are attracted by an elegant brown-stone structure inscribed with the words, "Young Women's Christian Association." I went in one evening. From the vestibule I am shown into the very pretty chapel, then into the vast sitting-room, which, with its comfortable seats, its sofas and its carpets, has all the appearance of a family parlor. I go up another story in the elevator, where I find the library and reading-rooms, containing all the newspapers and magazines. Here the scholars from the School of Design close by come to look for models; pieces of music and scores are lent gratuitously. There is a class in stenography and typewriting; there are also lessons in book-keeping. Adjoining the house, with a separate entrance, is the restaurant, — rooms well lighted and ventilated, where women employed all day in offices, schools, or studios find excellent meals at the lowest prices, served on small tables with the utmost neatness. Those whom I see look like ladies; yet there is a crowd, each having to wait her turn. I see one girl pay thirty cents for a dinner of five dishes, including coffee, — those tiny dishes which are all served at once, regardless of the fact that they will get cold, in all American hotels which are not on the European plan; they make one think of a Japanese bill of fare, or a doll's dinner. There is even a side dish, the ever-lasting ice-cream.

Connected with the buildings of the Christian Association is the Exchange for Woman's Work, which is nothing but a shop founded on charitable principles, and which exists in more or less flourishing condition in all American cities. Women of various conditions bring their work, which is sold anonymously, — needlework of every sort, from the finest to the coarsest; knitting, painted screens, lamp-shades, worsted-work, made-up linen, fans, all kinds of fancy articles and art wares. One of the best-stocked bazaars of this description which I saw was in Philadelphia ; pastry, preserves, cakes, and candies formed a large part of the trade. Orders are taken, whether for dinners, wedding outfits, wardrobes for babies, household linen, or mending ; every one feels it her duty to buy as much as possible. The Society take ten per cent of the amount of the sale, and the rest is sent to the anonymous work-woman, who is told, if she is not extremely skilful, to perfect herself in the trade-school belonging to the establishment, for only the most finished products are displayed. Private subscriptions pay for the rent, the lighting and heating, and other expenses of the house.

No, wealth in America is not without a soul.

I never felt more sure of this than when I visited those homes for workingmen which are not meant to be works of charity, but mere co-operative enterprises. Before describing them, let us see how hard and how costly it is to live in a great city; let us try to show the other side of the vast wealth displayed in the elegant quarters of New York. To do this we have only to take several elevated trains in succession, and to pass, as if borne by the crutch of Asmodeus, over those parts of the city which are not fashionable. We fly through the air upon a slender viaduct supported at intervals by iron posts. From a height varying from the second to the fourth floor, we gaze into a sort of reddish abyss, mottled with posters and signs, swarming with a countless mass of passers all in a hurry, all busy, walking rapidly, none of them looking about them. Besides, there is nothing to see, — nothing but the endless lines of tall red house-fronts, wearisome in their uniformity. With their ugly, ungainly front steps, they seem to say to the common people: "We have gone to no expense; this is good enough for poor folks. If they can't spend more than four or five hundred dollars for their rooms, so much the worse for them." It is impossible to tell one from another of these brick or sandstone faces without a shadow of expression or originality. Go down into one of these streets, and you will be astonished to see how carefully the number on each door is hidden instead of being made conspicuous as in France. The invisible janitor will show you how greatly misunderstood the good Parisian porter has been; and the dirty, ignorant, familiar Irish maid-servant, by comparison, will give you the highest idea of the humble maid of all work in the " old country." No doubt ordinary provisions, considering their wonderful abundance, are no dearer at market here than in Paris; but with such cooks, one is reduced to the daily steak, — always steak. If they know how to cook it properly, they consider themselves very skilful, and demand higher wages.

It is therefore easy to understand the preference for boarding shown by people who cannot spend a great deal. Rather than to keep house, they choose between refuges of various classes, — some being extremely elegant and others equally modest, — where food, heat, light, and service are provided in a lump for so much a month or a week. Such a resource is invaluable to women who have a career, from which they do not wish to be distracted by domestic cares. Now, in America these women are a legion. In the first place, there are the teachers in public schools; counting only these, there are

245,098 to 123,287 men teachers. Then there
are the women in the service of the government:
at Washington alone there are 6,105; elsewhere
2,104, not to mention the 6,285 post-mistresses.
How can such women be what we call " domestic "
women? I know that an eminent woman mathematician of Baltimore, Mrs. Christine Ladd Franklin, in her biography of Sophie Germain,[1] which
seems as if written by a Frenchwoman, protests
against the prejudice which requires a learned
woman to be *nothing but* a learned woman. She
is fully justified. Married to a mathematician, she
affords a most striking contradiction to all our antiquated ideas of rivalry between the sexes, at the
same time that she proves that the most abstract
studies are compatible with the duties of a wife and
mother. But she is the exception; she is purely
and simply an instance of admirable American
equipoise, which may be contrasted with the story
of a Sophie Kowalevsky.

As a general rule, life is too short to admit of so
many interests, so many contrary cares; and it is
for want of accepting this truth that people run the
risk of doing nothing thoroughly. Thus an American girl who was engaged to be married said to
me, as she announced her approaching marriage:

[1] " The Century Magazine," October, 1894.

" We will have a home of our own when our affairs permit." She wrote; her husband went to some office; each of them belonged to a club.

If the club and boarding-house are useful to all busy people who have not yet made a fortune, how much more necessary must they be to the working-classes! One often hears in New York of forewomen who are paid fifty dollars a week; of dressmakers and milliners who easily earn from two dollars and a half to three dollars a day in great houses which rival those of Paris. This may be. All artists are well paid in America, — the artist in dresses and hats as well as the rest. But not every one is an artist; there is the army of artisans. Do you know that a mere working-girl on the average receives but five dollars, or five dollars and a quarter, a week? Now, the lowest rents are tremendous; on the other hand, the tenement-house in the crowded districts is a den of vice and disease which defies all description. Situated in the midst of gambling hells, drinking saloons, and low-class dance halls, it affords its occupants but wretched lodgings, — so wretched that they may be tempted to seek refuge in the worst places merely that they may be warm. Therefore we can but pity the little working-girl who has no family, or who has left her family from that desire for independence which may be called a national characteristic. Her fate would be even worse, if help did not come from above, wholly impersonal, and so disguised that it cannot be confounded with alms.

Perhaps this feeling of solidarity which exists between rich and poor is more natural here than elsewhere in a society where great fortunes are made in the twinkling of an eye, and where many very wealthy people still have fresh in their memory their own years of privation. It is certain that one generous soul has only to take the initiative for a stream of gifts to flow in. Thanks to these gifts, a home suddenly rises in a respectable part of the town, — a large house amply warmed, with broad stairs leading to neat rooms, possibly to chambers with three or four beds in each, but neat and of generous size. Substantial meals are served at convenient hours. All this is at the disposal of working-girls; it costs them no more than the mean lodging. They have books besides; in case of sickness, they are taken care of. They are perfectly free: there is nothing to prevent them from receiving their friends, men and women, in a real parlor, where nothing is wanting, not even a piano; and where little parties are given regularly, the only rule being that they must be in by ten o'clock.

Who can wonder at the success of the homes for working-girls which are now so numerous in New York, although there are not enough yet? I visited several of them, with which I have but one fault to find, — that is, they give a poor girl habits which her future husband will find it very hard to keep up. The condition for admission to these homes is, in addition to blameless conduct, the fact of not earning more than a certain fixed sum. There are homes of all kinds, there is even one for ladies who earn their living by some form of literary labor. The Ladies' Christian Union, the mother house, in a fine part of the town, holds eighty-five boarders, and it is always full; the price of board supplies the table and housekeeping expenses, the other expenses being paid by the originators of the scheme. One branch of this house is especially devoted to shop-girls. There are even homes for the very young girls who pay their way by domestic labor. They learn to use the sewing-machine; they are taught laundry work and mending. Girls out of work may wait for a place in temporary homes at a low price. Primrose House is a home for convalescents, for lonely girls whose wages are too small to maintain them. If they earn a dollar a week, they are required to pay twenty-five cents; if they earn two dollars, fifty cents, and so on; when they get up to more than five dollars, they are requested to go to some other home. All clubs are also registry offices.

Other American cities have followed the example set by Miss Dodge. The excellent Boston Associations try to train servants, and care for unknown and friendless girls coming from a distance, sending their agents to steamboats and railroad stations to give advice and information to those who need them. Baltimore is perhaps the city where the different societies act together best to promote their useful work, — Protestant societies taking in the Catholics without a word of argument, and St. Vincent's Home throwing open its doors to Protestants with equal tolerance. Philadelphia, the Quaker City, on the contrary, is quite exclusive; but it is not to be outdone by any other city in generosity. Its New Century Guild of Working-Girls is famous. Hundreds of young girls go there for lessons in the manual arts; the time will soon come when it will be changed into a college of arts and trades, which in its way will be quite equal to the others. And the same pains are invariably taken with moral development, as is proved by the club which bears the odd name of "Once a Day Club." The members sign an agreement to do some service once a day, how-

ever small it may be, to some person whom they
are under no obligation to help. A night's shelter
on a vast scale is a part of some of these homes.
Restaurants for working-girls are often connected
with large dressing-rooms, which are much fre-
quented by shop-girls, who are often lodged in
crowded quarters.

In the West, there are such comfortable boarding-houses for shop-girls that many people of
quite a different class went to them from motives
of economy; and it was found necessary to establish rules to prevent this abuse. At St. Paul,
Minnesota, a Catholic lady, Miss J. Schley, with
a capital of $125, opened a home for young girls,
which has peculiar features to recommend it, being
the very abode of pleasure. The girls who live
there dance to the piano every evening; several
times during the winter, they invite their men
friends to small balls. These same young men
may also join the girls' literary club, which has
an evening of music and recitations once a fortnight. Nobody can join the society until they
have shown themselves capable of contributing
in some way to the amusement of the others; consequently dullards are left out, which cannot often
be said of fashionable circles. All over thirty
years of age, and all widows and divorced women

are also ineligible. These favorable conditions bring about many marriages; they are celebrated in the institution by a wedding feast given to the couple.

But I am really afraid of giving the idea that a Utopian existence is insured to American working-girls by the advance of sociology; this would be the very reverse of the truth. They struggle hard for their maintenance, in spite of the help given them by the churches and by individuals. However, their situation is improving daily, for the very reasons which have reduced so many men to the sad position of malcontents and unemployed. When the increasing and perfected intervention of machines renders the expenditure of human strength superfluous, the workman leaves to the work-woman that part of the work which requires only attention and skill. Of course, women are content with moderate wages. Women earn less than men in almost all branches, from teaching to manual labor; we protest against this injustice, but it has thus far been impossible to remedy it. Is it not something, after all, to have provided so many openings which only a few years ago did not exist? There are now three hundred and forty-three trades at which American women can work.

The Chinese are persistent rivals of the weaker sex even in those industries which would seem to be of right reserved for women.   The Chinese are marvellously skilful in housework, and have taken complete possession of that field in San Francisco. They steal into many factories where women are employed.   In New York they do a large part of the laundry work.   Are they indeed men, these hybrid and mysterious beings in costumes as puzzling as their sallow faces with their narrow eyes? A small round hat, loose trousers like a divided skirt, a sort of jacket, all of coarse blue cloth, an umbrella tucked under the arm, — such is the type which all Chinese copy so closely that it is hard to tell one from another in the cars and on boats. Their immobility is somewhat fantastic; hidden behind their big sleeves, they seem, like cats, to see nothing.   In the streets generally so ill-kept, and turned into rivers of mud whenever it rains, they move with feline speed, shod in thick-soled white slippers which never have the slightest stain. I met many Chinese men, but not one Chinese woman.   The negroes have children by the dozen; the Chinese, in spite of their reputation for multiplying, in New York seem to be all bachelors. Honest Yankee traders (I speak from hearsay) smuggle a few specimens of yellow femininity into the dens of Chinatown — a region scarcely to be commended — to be found in the populous Bowery, with the German, Italian, and Jewish quarters. At night, parti-colored lanterns swing over opium shops. These people, of very doubtful morality, are marvellously skilful and ingenious, and apparently succeed, in whatever country they may be, in living upon little or nothing.

But to come back to working-girls, the lot of the best of them is as much as possible improved by the solicitude of which they are the object. Women are not allowed to undertake work that is too heavy or tiresome. The European custom of permitting women to work in the fields like beasts of burden seems to Americans barbarous. The idea that women should be employed in mines is abhorrent. And yet the system of tobacco factories and cotton mills is hard enough in its way. Many little girls begin to work at twelve or thirteen; the usual age is fourteen. After the age of twenty-five, their number decreases: no doubt marriage is the cause of this. The name " working-girls " as applied to them is therefore correct; they are for the most part young girls.

Before leaving this subject, I desire to acknowledge the extreme courtesy with which I was received in Washington, in the office of the Department of

Labor, where official reports of priceless value, made up from investigations carried on by its agents in various cities, were placed at my service: women are supposed to appreciate what concerns their sex, better than men do. There were statistics carefully drawn up and ample details concerning the various trades, wages, and habits of working-women, the general condition of their life, etc. Even the question of morals is considered, — not thoroughly, which would be impossible, vice and misery having so many dark recesses, but from the standpoint of professional dissoluteness. This portion of the report, with other details relating to California, is only furnished by the masculine agents of the department. If we can trust their statements, it does not seem that regular prostitutes are recruited from the ranks of the working-girls. The majority of lost women come straight from the family home without any previous trade, unless it be that of servant, especially servants in hotels, who gradually sink lower and lower. Many of them are foreigners. Emigration, once the wealth of America, is now one of its sore spots. The scum of the European world now collects in the low quarters of large cities, and remains there.

DOMESTIC LIFE.

Has the American working-woman when married the same domestic qualities which exist in France among the same class? I hardly think so. At any rate, these qualities are not inborn with her, as they are with the Frenchwoman. When a committee of ladies interested in the lot of the young girls who crowd the tobacco and hat manufactories of Baltimore, opened a housekeeping school for their benefit, some four years ago, and undertook to teach them what a Baltimorean devoted heart and soul to the modern question of the advancement of woman — Miss Elizabeth King — does not hesitate to place in the first rank of duties, it was found necessary to begin at the very beginning. The poor creatures did not know how to sweep, or dust, or lay a table, or peel a potato. And almost all were pupils of the public schools, amply instructed in regard to far less important points! Miss King tells us that the rapid progress made, by which the family table in many a laborer's home benefited, made the cooking classes very popular. The girls came every day at the close of their grammar school, tired though they were after studying all day, to beg for a lesson. A happy

compromise was finally made between the cooking
and the grammar schools. As Miss King most
justly says, primary and secondary education cannot be considered a success until the knowledge
gained is applied where the demand for it is universally felt, — in the household. May all reformers throughout the universe become converted to
her opinion! No one then need fear that the
" woman question " moves too rapidly.

There is just now an attempt in America to elevate in the esteem of woman that neglected realm,
the household, by labelling it " domestic science."
Domestic science is taught, as I have already stated,
in public schools and Christian Associations. Girls
thus learn to do systematically those things otherwise done heedlessly and somewhat at haphazard.
The reason for everything is given, the nutritive
qualities of each article of diet are explained, the
anatomy of the animal is the subject of study, as
are also the action of water and heat in the pre-
paration of food. It remains to be seen whether
pedantry be not a dangerous element: an old pro-
verb of the country best acquainted with the subject
tells us that good cooks are born not made. Be
this as it may, the important point is to rouse
by any means a spirit of emulation among American women in this field, which is not to their taste.

The facilities offered by boarding-houses, clubs, and restaurants have utterly destroyed in many of them those qualities which we are in the habit of regarding as pre-eminently those of their sex. The result is that the almost imperceptible machinery whose working is such a matter of course in France that we scarcely think of it, is wanting in almost all homes where dollars do not abound.

We certainly meet with many excellent house-mistresses in the United States, not only among those who have a French cook, an English coachman, and pay their maid thirty dollars a month, but even among those of secondary rank, who in order to avoid constant domestic changes, and to keep up at least an appearance of what we call "easy circumstances," spend more than would be necessary in France to obtain luxury. In the small towns and remote villages of the Eastern States undegenerate heiresses of old Puritan traditions recall the fact that their ancestresses, descendants of the best families of the English middle classes, did their own work and practised that thriftiness which is now regarded as meanness. But you nowhere find that cunningly disguised industry which enables the Parisian woman to cut a good figure at a very moderate cost. The extravagant price of all superfluities prevents this;

and so does a repugnance to stoop to duties which
may as well be called by their true name, — those
of the husband's servant maid. The American
woman of to-day, whether she be an operative or
an artisan, will resolutely deny that such is her
destiny in this world; she considers that it is quite
as much the man's place to take care of the baby, to
go to market, etc., as it is hers. Rough tasks are
not for her. It is men who do the selling in the
market stalls. You will never see a woman sitting
at the desk in the butcher shop or the grocery
belonging to her husband, helping him, ready to
assume the intelligent charge of the business if
the head of the house should be called away. No;
the father of the family, be he a millionnaire or only
a poor fellow, must provide for his wife's wants.
If she chooses to work too, it is usually in some
wholly different direction. She will not be a partner, a humble satellite; she must fly with her own
wings wherever it seems good to her.

It is natural that a people who earn so much
and spend so much should scorn the petty con-
trivance of that economy which in France is
encouraged. The epithet "mean," the most in-
sulting of all, would speedily be applied to them.
Waste, on the contrary, is synonymous in America with magnificence. In hotels, the orders

given to the men, black or white, who wait on
the table, seem to be that they are to ruin and
to lose everything.   In private houses the servants are but too often possessed of the same
purpose.   And how hard it is to find and to keep
those servants, bad as they are!   To expect any
affection from them would be presumptuous.   The
general love of travelling prevents this.   Masters
dismiss their servants as easily as the latter quit
them.   With equal indifference, many people of
ample means let their town or country house to
strangers, during an absence of greater or less
duration.   They are surprised that they cannot in
the same way find a furnished house in France,—
some hereditary castle or other to let for a couple
of seasons., And we cannot make them understand our dislike for this sort of thing, — a dislike
as unknown to the English as it is to the Americans, two nations who pride themselves on being
the only people who understand the meaning of
" home," for which they say we have no word!

The problem of domestic life which exists everywhere in America, and which can only be solved
by large supplies of money, becomes even more
complicated in the Western States.   One of my
first surprises in Chicago was the singular lecture
given by a Denver lady, Mrs. Coleman Stuckert,

upon a plan of her invention which would simplify
matters amazingly. To illustrate her discourse,
she first unrolled a series of plans and architectural
drawings, representing houses of all dimensions
and all prices, in ultra-composite styles which she
dubbed Venetian, Roman, Spanish, and I know
not what all. These structures placed at the service of the best-lined purses and within the reach
also of the scantiest, were to form a species of
city provided with all the modern instruments
furnished by steam and electricity, with wagons
swift as lightning depositing from door to door
the meals ordered at the headquarters of the Association, — meals simple or magnificent as desired,
the fortunate inhabitants having to take no trouble,
save to pick up the manna apparently dropped
from heaven. In the centre of the square surrounded by these separate dwellings were luxurious
buildings common to all, where any one could at
pleasure engage a ball-room, arrange a banquet,
or give any kind of an entertainment. Comfort,
economy, varied resources both material and intellectual, from a library to a gymnasium, — nothing was wanting to the families thus united in a
co-operative society, without any inconvenient contact, without any occasion for acquaintance unless
they desired it. The realization of such a scheme

would be a decisive step toward the dreams of
the year 2000 as conceived by Mr. Bellamy, whose
book, by the way, seems, upon a second reading in
the United States, far less fantastic than when opened
in France for the first time.   Mrs. Coleman Stuckert interested me by her fervent convictions, her
prodigious fluency, by all that she told us of her
own experiences as a house-mistress and as the
mother of a family in the Queen City of the plains,
which, according to Hepworth Dixon, did not contain a single woman in 1866, and which now has
one hundred and fifty thousand inhabitants!   It
is her intention to visit Europe, to exhibit economic
plans destined, she says, to meet with universal
success.   It would have been useless for me to
tell her that Europeans are not accustomed to
associations; that however republican the French
may have become they still keep servants; and
that we still distrust, being prejudiced persons,
sauces made all at once and for so many people.
I therefore confined myself to compliments.   She
will have to be quick about getting out a patent,
for it struck me, in travelling through the different
States, that her idea had also occurred to others,
with improvements of various sorts, — a certain
pneumatic tube, for instance, through which dinners could be despatched like so many letters or

telegrams, would be an advantageous exchange
for the provision wagon, electric though it be. ´

All these projects, received with favor, at least
in theory, show a growing tendency, in spite of
the success of cooking schools, to rest content
with boarding-house and hotel life more or less
disguised. The Frenchwoman would never be
satisfied with it, because she clings, poor as she
may be, to her home. But we must remember
that an American woman, rich though she may
be, thoroughly loves all sorts of camp life. She
enjoys herself in summer in a Saratoga caravan-
sary, where two thousand beds are at the service
of those who drink the waters, where everything
is vast and splendid. In town she likes to invite
her friends to a restaurant. I saw the girls known
as " bachelor girls " call for the bill of fare as
naturally as if they were bachelors indeed. An
amiable Philadelphian who took me to her club,
where she graciously put me down as a temporary
member, explained its advantages. " It 's very convenient," she said, " when my husband is away.
Then I breakfast here; I make appointments with
my friends; I find the newspapers. There are
even bedrooms for those of us who may want to
come in for a day or two from the country." And
yet the lady who said this was one of the most

accomplished house-mistresses whom I met in America, making very good use, as is the custom as we go farther South, of colored people as servants.

Liberal as the North prides itself on being, it has a horror of familiar contact with negroes. Their transient service seems acceptable on rail-road trains and steamboats, in certain hotels, etc., the more so since they are generally very attentive and very assiduous; but tolerance stops there. It is not until we reach Baltimore that this feeling disappears for good and all. Baltimoreans and Washingtonians do not yet go so far as to pray in the same church with the race of Ham; but they employ them in the kitchen, the stable, and the house, and it seems to me that they do well. The negro is moulded by his surroundings. Left to himself, he may be the most disagreeable of brutes; placed with vulgar people, he becomes as familiar and as insolent as they; but with good masters, he is often the most perfect of servants. I never tasted better cooking than that of a good black cook in the South. She does not require, for the development of this sort of genius, the special classes where young Northern girls condescend to study an inferior branch of chemistry with the aid of all the perfect machinery which does away with drudgery. The negress proves that intuition is superior to method when it comes to seasoning; she may become a *cordon bleu emeritus* in the hands of one of those house-mistresses such as are to be found in New Orleans, who, vying with the most famous gastronomers of France, scorn canned food, crackers, and other "educational" biscuit, and the more or less adulterated food products lauded by American puffery. Nowhere in the world can better cooking be found than in Louisiana. The South has not yielded in this respect to the influences of its victor; it evidently retains the French traditions of early days, which Creole spices and flavorings are far from injuring. Appetizing odors always escape from the humblest negro cabin; it is quite the reverse in Northern country homes. A landscape painter, who had returned to New York after a long stay in France, declared to me his intention of going back, not only because he despaired of subjecting to the exigencies of art the American country, which lacks details, and which at its finest moment is of so gaudy a splendor, but more especially because his stomach could not endure the fare provided by the country inns. O Barbizon! O Marlotte! O Douarnenez! O humble paradise of artists! How you were regretted, you and your peasants, in head-kerchiefs or in caps, who unfailingly hand down from generation to generation the secret of making an omelette and stewing a rabbit! There are no caps and no head-kerchiefs, there are no peasants, in the United States. At a football match between two villages in the State of Maine, I saw the crowd of rustics, similar at every point to a crowd of middle class citizens and gathered together, moreover, for a kind of sport which is the favorite amusement of all classes alike. The football game between Harvard and Yale filled the newspapers for almost a week. The country game no doubt had less solemnity about it, but there was quite as much animation and spirit on the part of both players and spectators, there being plenty of women among the latter. The players, handsome youths, in their fighting gear, as soon as the game was over, put on hideous overcoats which gave them a horribly common air. The pretty country damsels were quite as elegant as the city working-girls, who wear the latest fashions and often quite expensive materials, furs and jewels; why not, if they like to spend all they earn on dress? A Philadelphia lady told me that she felt obliged to request her maidservant not to wait at table with diamonds in her ears!

"It is my pleasure to wear my fortune about me," quietly answered the girl.

"And it is my right to dismiss you," replied her mistress.

We must remember that the class of servants has not existed in the United States more than two hundred years. American women once gloried in looking after their houses; but those primitive days are long past. They correspond to the time when women were not permitted to teach, and only showed their capacity in this direction in Sunday Schools. America was then poor; with riches came a train of wants and of idle moments. There must be "help," assistants, who at first were the equals of their mistresses (let us take the word in the sense of "protectress," which is the true one), and were treated as such; that is, as members of the family. There followed very simple, very patriarchal customs, worthy of a republic. Then the flood of Irish emigration changed everything: the "help," who were often literary also, thanks to the excellent public schools, vanished before the invasion. Now Italians bid fair to replace the Irish as servants, the latter going into politics; the Italians are content with lower wages, and live more temperately. What has become of the "help" of former days? They are employed in business or in trade, as stenographers, typewriters, journalists, "interviewers" perhaps. The rage for the human document is carried to excess, almost to madness in America. Hundreds of women, to say nothing of men, lie in wait for every passer, to take him metaphorically by the throat, to wrest from him the latest news, sensational subjects, — sometimes to invent things that he never said, to arrange, in any case, and to complete in their own way, and to give the needful savor to the real conversation. How many feminine interviewers I have seen who were very superior to their profession, and who may have had a college diploma in their pockets!

Myriads of women write, some with talent; but teaching is the refuge of the great majority. The Normal Schools in thirty-eight States number twenty-three thousand pupils, and of these seventy-one per cent are women. Try to send back this swarm of women, set free by work, to the petty tasks of the household! Only try to prove to the least interesting of them that it is better to make a pretty gown, or to cook a dainty dish, than to produce poor literary work, and above all to do reporting! The superiority which permits one to recognize that the humblest things may be made as noble as the highest, by the way in which they are done, is very rare in every land. And what they particularly desire to establish is the absolute equality of the sexes. I heard an eminent woman seriously boast of a certain industrial school where the boys were taught a little sewing and the girls a little carpentry! These are exaggerations, from which they will recover.

INDUSTRIAL SCHOOLS. — AGRICULTURAL INSTITUTE AT HAMPTON.

Following in the train of the rich citizens who have lavished largess upon colleges, there already arise other benefactors whose no less splendid legacies and gifts flow into quite a different channel, — that of industrial education. It is but a few years since its advantages were recognized, but the public mind is already beginning to be pretty generally occupied with it. Possibly the mediocrity of many so called universities which have sprung up at random among genuine ones, possibly also their disadvantages, which consist in lending, as some one has very aptly said, large names to little things, have done much to bring about this reaction. In Philadelphia I visited Drexel Institute, named for its founder, — one hundred and fifty thousand dollars just sufficed to pay for the building and splendid fitting up of the edifice. It was opened to both sexes in 1891, and already has fifteen hundred pupils. All aptitudes for the various professional studies are developed by excellent classes, where applied mathematics, designing, natural science, and mechanics find a place. Drexel Institute, moreover, contains very rich collections of all sorts, which make it a school of æsthetics very precious in a land where public taste is not yet fully formed. No doubt recent exhibitions have led to very happy results in this particular. They have brought France into the foreground: educators invariably allude to France when they wish to praise the meaning of form and grace. Nevertheless, it is a great disadvantage for a people not to have constantly before them the monuments and masterpieces of every sort, daily contact with which teaches even the most ignorant of the French to understand beauty without comment or explanation. Until now it was a privileged class alone who profited by the raids made upon Europe for the purpose of filling up the museums and galleries of great cities. Thanks to professional schools, art studies will be universally spread abroad, gradually modifying too purely practical and utilitarian traits. The vast gymnasium, one of the striking features of Drexel Institute, is, in accordance with the founder's idea, used to promote this advance. I observed a singular detail, — photographs of students, a young man and woman, in a state of complete nudity, representing the average of their fellow students. This is an application of the discoveries of modern science to Greek art, which America claims to have inspired. The Greeks elevated a feeling for beauty into a form of worship; they saw beauty not only in images carved from marble or stone, but in the perfect forms of youth developed by the national games. This is the reason for this exhibition, which some might think indecent. It has also a useful purpose, — the physical progress gained by the use of the trapeze, the dumb-bells and the latest Swedish apparatus can thus be compared from year to year. But how far we are from the old Puritan spirit!

It is in the South that schools of arts and trades have grown most rapidly during the last twenty-five years. It was found necessary, after the war, to furnish some means of subsistence to the thousands of negroes suddenly set free by a single stroke of the pen, and at the same time to raise them by a certain amount of intellectual culture to the level of their new rank as American citizens, which nothing had prepared them to hold.

One of the men who from the first devoted himself most zealously to the work of reconstruction was General Armstrong, the founder of Hampton Institute (Normal and Agricultural). He had in his veins the blood of the missionary and the pedagogue: his father, one of the first Americans who went forth to preach the Gospel to the Sandwich Islands, was made minister of public instruction by the king of Hawaii. Even before he returned to the United States to finish his education, young Armstrong saw that the advance of piety among people almost innocently licentious is as nothing if it does not serve as the basis for the formation of character. He also noted that the Mission School, a purely elementary and professional school, did far more good in Hawaii than the government schools, whose aims were much more ambitious. These memories helped him, when he undertook to elevate the negroes, who by certain impulsive and childish traits reminded him of the natives among whom his childhood was passed.

During the war of secession, Samuel Armstrong commanded colored troops; he was struck by their obedience to discipline, by their devotion to officers who treated them well, and by their eagerness and dash in battle. He saw black soldiers studying the alphabet beside the camp-fire, and concluded that they must be given every possible chance to become like other men. Amid the

changing fortunes of a long and bloody struggle, he seemed to have a vision of the duty
which awaited him; and circumstances served him
strangely well. Being given charge of ten coun-
ties in Virginia, to settle negro affairs and regulate
the relations between the two races, he made his
headquarters at Hampton, close by Old Point Comfort, where the first pioneers landed in 1608, where
the first cargo of slaves was disembarked, where the
first Indian was baptized. In sight of these shores
the decisive battle between the " Merrimac " and
the " Monitor " was fought; at this point General
Grant settled the plan for his final campaign. General Armstrong judged that a place filled with
historic and strategic memories, easily accessible,
both from the North and the South, both by water
and by rail, destined to great commercial and mari-
time growth, situated in the best conditions for
health, might well be chosen as the home of the
school of his dreams.[1]

Already, directly after the war, a noble colored
woman, Mrs. Mary Peake, had gathered about her,
on the site of Camp Hamilton, where six thousand
dead now rest in a national cemetery, hundreds of
black children, the first school for free negroes, estab-

[1] Twenty-two Years' Work. Hampton Normal School Press,
1893.

lished with the help of the Missionary Association.
This same Association largely aided General Armstrong in the purchase of a vast estate on Hampton
River, and then requested him to become the head
of the Institute.   He had never dreamed, in his great
modesty, of doing more than suggesting and helping, not of directing; but he was ready for the
work, which began on a very small scale, in 1868,
with two teachers and fifteen scholars.   The number only too quickly increased.   Old ambulance
barracks which had been abandoned were per-
force turned into dormitories and workshops, while
they waited for the funds, which were not long in
coming, — the government having, in the mean
time, appropriated three millions and a half for
the education of a million colored children.   The
chief institutions, now prospering, had already been
thrown open.   Hampton received fifty thousand
dollars, as her share, and the necessary buildings
were put up.   In 1870, a special act of the General
Assembly of Virginia secured the incorporation of
the new school, declaring it independent of any association and of any sect, as well as of the government.   "Self-help" was its motto; it desired no
control.

General Armstrong's ideas at first found but
few partisans; but little faith was felt in manual

labor, the plea being that it would not bring in enough. It brought in a great deal from a moral standpoint, by rehabilitating labor, which had been degraded by slavery. " Like all men," said Armstrong, " the negro is what his past has made him." The general's purpose was, to exorcise that past, to remedy the influences of heredity and surroundings, to test character, for the promotion of which he cared ten thousand times more than he did for remunerative and intelligent work; then to send out a select number to preach by word and by example. To this end he devoted his noble life; and he died last year content, asking that he might have the simple funeral of a soldier, a place in the school cemetery with his students, without distinction of any kind, with no eulogy over his grave. Some of his last words were: " I do not care for a biography; . . . they never tell the whole truth. The truth of a life is hidden deep within us; . . . we scarce know it ourselves, but God knows it. I have faith in His mercy. . . . Hampton has been a blessing to me; it has given me for friends and helpers the best of my fellow-citizens; and it was a happy fortune to be able to do some good to that whole race set free by the war; to be able also indirectly to serve the vanquished. . . . Few men have been so happy as I. I have never been called to make any sacrifice. It seems as if I had been guided in everything. Prayer is the great power in this world; it keeps us close to God. My prayers were weak and inconstant; but they were the best that I had. And now I am eager to see another world. No doubt everything there will be perfectly natural. How can any one fear death? It is a friend. God and country first, ourselves last."

This outline of General Armstrong's sentiments may be of use as showing what his influence was upon some one hundred and fifty thousand students of both sexes, — counting those of all the schools founded by Hampton graduates after the pattern of the mother school, in Alabama, Virginia, and North Carolina. Other pupils of the Institute, both men and women, are doing missionary work in Florida, Kentucky, South Carolina, and Texas. At Hampton itself there are now six hundred and fifty pupils between the ages of eighteen and twenty-eight, under the care of eighty officers and instructors, half of whom are divided among the various industrial departments. Does it not seem marvellous that among boys and girls of that age and race, living in separate buildings no doubt, but meeting constantly at meals, in class-rooms, at various meetings, no scandal has ever occurred?

Are we to believe that the presence of so just a man as Samuel Armstrong acted upon them as the very shadow of the divine presence?

The task of the Rev. H. B. Frissell, who has succeeded the founder, will be most difficult, although a decided impulse has already been given to the work. The progress made is extraordinary, even from a physical point of view; the ravages of consumption are greatly lessened, nervous affections, once very common, are now relatively rare and there is seldom a case of hysteria since the scholars have learned that a certain want of balance is considered the characteristic feature of their race. A very distinguished woman doctor lives at the Institute.

The annual cost of Hampton is one hundred thousand dollars, the work of the students being deducted. This sum is covered by the subsidies granted by Congress and by private gifts. America has ceased to count the sacrifices required to educate the negro: the thousands of free schools opened in the South for their benefit, require of the old Slave States an annual tax of very nearly four million dollars. The North supports twenty colleges, most of which are under the charge of churches, and at which five thousand adults are prepared for liberal careers; the women make their mark as teachers.

At New Orleans I saw a black damsel teaching Latin with great authority to a class of gentlemen of the same color: her short woolly hair carefully twisted into a correct knot, a little embroidered handkerchief thrust into her belt, a flower in her button-hole, she affected Boston ways. I also saw a class of little negro girls with faces like monkeys, studying Greek, and the disgust expressed by their former masters seemed to me quite justified. Free though I am from any prejudice against color, I consider the classes in sewing, cooking and laundry work established by good General Armstrong far more useful. He also encouraged floriculture and trained women gardeners. Nurses, of great renown in the neighborhood, are sent out from the little hospital in the Institute grounds. This practical knowledge does not prevent, quite the contrary, the Hampton students from being in great request as primary and religious teachers of children. Almost all of them teach, no matter what their real profession may be. In time we shall probably find women in the majority among teachers of colored schools as is the case with white schools. The men will make a specialty of various trades, having a turn for mechanics and singular skill with their fingers. All trades are taught them at Hampton, although General

282

THE CONDITION OF WOMAN

Armstrong particularly favored agriculture and although preparing timber is the chief business.

Perhaps the excellent spirit of this model Institute may exorcise some of the perils caused by the presence in America of eight millions of individuals who never asked to go there, but who cannot be driven forth. Negroes properly trained will find fresh outlets, and above all they will benefit by the best of moral gymnastics, that which consists in earning all that they spend, in working with their hands all day in order to enjoy the privilege of studying at night, even if it take years and years to gain a laborious victory over the longed for knowledge. Some students, after following a trade abroad, return, and that more than once, to the school-room benches. These young men, it seems to me, assert the growth of the black race better than they could do by great talents. Such perseverance and energy are worth more than the higher education gained at the universities of Howard and Lincoln, Fisk and Atlanta, an education, by the way, which, if it give him other rights, does not insure to the grandson of a slave possessing it either the privilege of entering a drawing-room or that of a seat in a box at a theatre. He is assigned a place fitting his social rank, even on railroads, where we are told that there are no first or second classes, but where you will invariably see this insolent distinction, — "waiting room for colored people."

"Only in the South!" some one may say.

Allow me to give an idea of the feeling in the North on this point, to repeat an anecdote told with much spirit by Mr. Marshall, one of the managers of Hampton. Boston having proved by gifts the interest which she took in the success of the Agricultural Institute, it was decided that a meeting should be held in that city on January 27, 1870: General Armstrong was to go there in company with a negro orator, named Langston. The latter arrived first, at night, at the Parker House. When the hotel-keeper found out next day, to his disgust, that he had a colored man in the house, he made up his mind, without the least hesitation, to turn him out: unfortunately the chief notabilities of the city came to visit the pariah, just at that very moment; the order could not be carried out until they had taken their departure; but others came and so many of them that the opportunity to turn the negro out of doors was lost, but Mr. Langston is the first colored man who ever entered the Parker House as a guest. The same state of things exists in the restaurants, and the waiters came near taking by the collar "the negro"

who afterwards became United States minister
to Hayti.

Even now, in the liberal town of Boston, see
whether the lightest colored mulatto, unless he be
some celebrity or lion, will dare take advantage of
the rights theoretically granted to him.   Imagine
a negro, even if he were a great man, aspiring to
the hand of a white woman, in the East!   He
would be dismissed with scorn to the Southern
ladies, whose reply, gracious and attractive though
they may be, would have all the ferocity of an
application of lynch law;   now we know with
what refinements of cruelty that savage law
punishes a negro guilty of pursuing a white
woman to the last extreme.   We have only to
refer to the recent, shocking examples of which
the West was the scene.

From North to South and from East to West,
the negro is only tolerated in the United States
on condition that he keeps his place, and it will
become very difficult to determine the place where
a man is to remain who in education and career is
equal to the most distinguished.   A solid primary
education, then an industrial education therefore
seems to be what is most to be desired for the
colored population, in their own interest; General Armstrong saw this, although he opened the

way for exceptions resolved on rising to greater heights, at any cost, even that of suffering. Carefully kept records show the work accomplished by his scholars scattered through the world, from mere laborers to ministers of the Gospel, lawyers, government clerks, and artists (there are quite a number of musicians).

If I have omitted to say that out of the six hundred and fifty pupils at Hampton, one hundred and thirty-two are Indians, it is because I intend to speak later of the admirable school at Carlisle, where they are to be found in crowds, with no mixture of negro fellow-pupils. " The friend of the Indians," Miss Alice Fletcher, shall introduce my readers to them, as she really did me. Without the explanations kindly given me by this charitable and learned woman, upon the subject to which she devotes her life, I should but feebly have understood the beauty of the work of Capt. R. H. Pratt, the rival of General Armstrong, we may say his associate in the work of elevating the " despised races."

www.ingramcontent.com/pod-product-compliance
Lightning Source LLC
Chambersburg PA
CBHW030342270326
41926CB00009B/923